"Ebony Small has written an extraordinary book about her transformational journey in Christ. From New York City to the world, Ebony writes with great transparency and thoughtfulness. Be inspired."

Mac Pier, founder of Movement.org

"I am proud to call Ebony Small a friend. Few young leaders have the intellectual, spiritual, and social qualities Ebony exhibits, and fewer still have the ability to share what they have learned quite so effectively. In *The Leader in You* Ebony uses her life story to share deep, practical advice on how all of us can become more useful tools in building the kingdom. We are all leaders in one way or another, and I am grateful that God raises up amazing young leaders like Ebony so that we can all become more effective."

Kevin Palau, president and CEO of the Luis Palau Association

"Ebony Small shares personal experiences that led to a transformational understanding of God's revealed purpose for her life. She also deftly weaves in examples of leaders—from men and women of biblical history to twenty-first-century visionaries in ministry, business, and entertainment—whose lives illustrate her insight on leadership development. *The Leader in You* also poses reflection questions that will inspire and empower emerging leaders committed to pursuing a God-honoring life."

Michael G. Scales, president of Nyack College and Alliance Theological Seminary

"Ebony Small is my friend and one of the most dynamic voices rising up in the church today. In an age of same-old leadership models and advice, *The Leader in You* offers a prophetic word from someone who can relate with anyone who feels they don't quite fit the mold. If you are seeking to find your place in God's movement, this book is for you. There is a generation waiting to be unleashed, and I believe *The Leader in You* could be the catalyst."

Nick Hall, chief communicator and founder of PULSE

"Ebony Small takes us through an inspiring journey of learning readily applicable leadership techniques while sharing her personal story of spiritual growth and leadership development. She provides a helpful roadmap for discovering the type of leader you are and applying it to multiple areas of your life. Read this book to understand yourself more and become a better leader."

Justin Tennison, president of PULSE

"In a time when leadership scholarship ca  ʌords match her walk. This necessary resource ʿom a woman who has blazed many trails and i fts. If you are questioning your courage to lea꜀ ꜱ, this book is for you!"

Nicole Martin, director of United States ministry for the Amᴇʀɪᴄᴀɴ ʙ...

"Two key words come to mind as I read *The Leader in You*: *humility* and *integrity*. The author shares her insights, gained through myriad experiences, with such transparency and authenticity that readers are sure to be rewarded."

Carlton T. Brown, senior pastor of Bethel Gospel Assembly, New York City

"*The Leader in You* is about Ebony Small's life . . . and your life! Ebony invites us into the 'God story' of her life, revealing—with vulnerability, humility, and insight—how God has not wasted a single marker in her life for his greater purpose. And *The Leader in You* is about God's story in you! With wisdom and practicality, Ebony invites each of us to live courageously in discovering God's grander purpose for our life. Prepare for life change!"

Craig Sider, president and CEO of Movement.org

"Ebony Small's emergence as a leading voice in her generation flows from deep wells of discernment and wisdom. In *The Leader in You* she shares how our meeting God's process of calling and shaping us as leaders with openness and obedience positions us for surprising outcomes. Regardless of the level of influence to which you are called, this book will bless you."

Claude Alexander, senior pastor, The Park Ministries, Charlotte, North Carolina

"*The Leader in You* allows the reader to feel understood, exhorted, admonished, and encouraged, all at the same time. I recommend it highly!"

Jazmin L. Montes, pastor at Community Christian Center, Staten Island

"I am so blessed to know Ebony personally, and I am perpetually inspired by her life, her leadership, and now her new book, *The Leader in You*. She possesses the unique skill set to navigate the complicated landscape of leadership dynamics while walking the reader through the process of self-discovery. Ebony's ability to thrive in the midst of urban and suburban, young and not-so-young, church, nonprofits, and the social sector is fully put on display through the anointing evident on her life and her writing."

Adam Durso, New York City Mayor's Clergy Advisory Council and executive director of LEAD. NYC

"It's not often that a young author inspires readers to consider the role they can play to advance God's kingdom. Ebony's book is for all who seek to maximize their leadership potential. Her experiences and story will empower and guide you to be your best self in response to a higher calling."

Wanji Walcott, chief legal officer at Discover Financial Services

"*The Leader in You* belongs in the hand of anyone with a sincere heart desiring to lead and to be led from a place of truth. Using lessons from her personal journey, testimonials, and biblical examples, Pastor Small illustrates the powerful, unimaginable ways in which God blesses and uses His leaders to fulfill divine purpose. This book will lighten the burden of equipping leaders and provide training for the saints who dare to struggle with the call to leadership."

Chermain Lashley, pastor of Grace United Methodist Church of St. Albans, New York

"Pastor Ebony has beautifully penned the road to transformational mentoring. Because her writing is so authentic, we not only witness her journey but receive concrete steps, courage, and hope for our own leadership journey. . . . *The Leader in You* is a must-read for anyone called to mentor the 'now' and 'next' generations."

Annette H. Cutino, director of Advance, LEAD.NYC

THE LEADER IN YOU

DISCOVERING YOUR
UNEXPECTED PATH
TO INFLUENCE

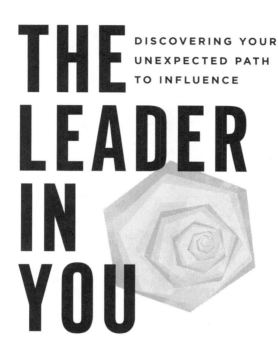

EBONY S. SMALL

An imprint of InterVarsity Press
Downers Grove, Illinois

InterVarsity Press
P.O. Box 1400, Downers Grove, IL 60515-1426
ivpress.com
email@ivpress.com

InterVarsity Press® is the book-publishing division of InterVarsity Christian Fellowship/USA®, a movement of students and faculty active on campus at hundreds of universities, colleges, and schools of nursing in the United States of America, and a member movement of the International Fellowship of Evangelical Students. For information about local and regional activities, visit intervarsity.org.

All Scripture quotations, unless otherwise indicated, are taken from The Holy Bible, New International Version®, NIV®. Copyright © 1973, 1978, 1984, 2011 by Biblica, Inc.™ Used by permission of Zondervan. All rights reserved worldwide. www.zondervan.com. The "NIV" and "New International Version" are trademarks registered in the United States Patent and Trademark Office by Biblica, Inc.™

While any stories in this book are true, some names and identifying information may have been changed to protect the privacy of individuals.

Cover design and image composite: David Fassett
Interior design: Daniel van Loon
Images: abstract pattern: © Liyao Xie / Moment Collection / Getty Images
         painted abstract: © Qweek / E+ / Getty Images
         abstract watercolor: © oxygen / Moment Collection / Getty Images

ISBN 978-0-8308-3183-8 (print)
ISBN 978-0-8308-3184-5 (digital)

Printed in the United States of America ♾

Library of Congress Cataloging-in-Publication Data
Names: Small, Ebony S., 1979- author.
Title: The leader in you : discovering your unexpected path to influence / Ebony S. Small.
Description: Downers Grove, Illinois : InterVarsity Press, an imprint of InterVarsity Press, 2020. | Includes bibliographical references.
Identifiers: LCCN 2020008011 (print) | LCCN 2020008012 (ebook) | ISBN 9780830831838 (print) | ISBN 9780830831845 (digital)
Subjects: LCSH: Leadership—Religious aspects—Christianity.
Classification: LCC BV4597.53.L43 S63 2020 (print) | LCC BV4597.53.L43 (ebook) | DDC 253—dc23
LC record available at https://lccn.loc.gov/2020008011
LC ebook record available at https://lccn.loc.gov/2020008012
A catalog record for this book is available from the Library of Congress.

| P | 25 | 24 | 23 | 22 | 21 | 20 | 19 | 18 | 17 | 16 | 15 | 14 | 13 | 12 | 11 | 10 | 9 | 8 | 7 | 6 | 5 | 4 | 3 | 2 | 1 |
| Y | 37 | 36 | 35 | 34 | 33 | 32 | 31 | 30 | 29 | 28 | 27 | 26 | 25 | 24 | 23 | 22 | 21 | 20 |

TO MY HEAVENLY FATHER

You've given me a new life and purpose.
I am because of you.

TO MY PARENTS

Thank you for loving and believing
in me no matter what!

TO MY SIBLINGS AND GODCHILDREN

I live to make you proud.

TO LINDA

This book is what it is because of your wisdom.
"Thank you" is not enough.

CONTENTS

HOW GOD SHAPES US

We say with confidence,
"The Lord is my helper; I will not be afraid.
What can mere mortals do to me?"

HEBREWS 13:6

UP UNTIL THE FOURTH GRADE I was bullied by two girls at my school in East Harlem. Let's call them Sarah and Christine. I don't know what made me a target. All I wanted was to make it stop.

I was a quiet kid. I loved school. I was one of the lucky students who won a school lottery to study the violin under the instruction of Ms. Roberta Guaspari, the subject of the film *Music of the Heart*.

Sarah, Christine, and I were in the same class. Sarah and Christine were best friends. They were bigger than I was. I felt powerless against them and their endless teasing. All I wanted was friendship and to be loved. I was desperate to fit in.

I told my mom that I was being bullied. She encouraged me to stand up to both girls and assured me that I would see them for who they were—all bark and no bite.

One day during recess Sarah threatened to slap me. I was terrified. I didn't want to be beaten up. But then I remembered my mom's instruction: "Just stand up to her." I would see what she was really made of.

When Sarah said again that she would slap me, I responded, "Do it!" I was stunned as the words left my mouth. Where did this boldness come from?

Sarah was shocked. I had never stood up for myself before. We had a standoff/stare down that felt like it lasted for an eternity. She kept gesturing as if she was going to slap me. We got closer and closer to each other, faces nearly touching.

I kept saying over and over again, "Do it!"

Finally, she backed off. I couldn't believe it!

That day, something changed in me.

This experience became just one of the markers that led to my discovery of the person God called me to be: a leader who deals with people who are terrified, overwhelmed, angry, hopeless, oppressed, and in need of deliverance. Just as I needed someone to speak into my life when I was a kid, people today need leaders to speak into their lives.

REMEMBER WHO YOU ARE

If you saw the 1994 animated movie *The Lion King* or the Broadway play of that name, you remember Simba's struggle to be a leader. Believing himself to be responsible for the death of his father Mufasa, he ran away from his family at Pride Rock. Though he found companionship with Pumbaa and Timon, who became his surrogate parents, he forgot who he was—the son of the king of all of the animals. While he was away, his people suffered under the cruel rulership of his uncle Scar. Simba needed to be reminded of who he was and what he had to do. Maybe that's where you are today.

Have you ever been in trials or battles so intense that you lost sight of who you were? Maybe you started to believe the things being said about you. Maybe you thought they were right about you. Perhaps you thought, *Maybe I am unqualified. Maybe I can't overcome in this area.*

In 2006, I worked at Memorial Sloan-Kettering Cancer Center (MSKCC) as an associate director for special programs in the development department. My responsibilities included planning the newly launched "Rock-And-Run on the River," a 5K run/walk event, as well as supporting external organizations sponsoring fundraising events on behalf of the hospital. Six months into my new role, my boss began to criticize my work performance after previously lauding me for such great work. Her disdain for me seemed sudden and soon became unbearable. There were days when I would go into the bathroom, get on my hands and knees in the stall, and cry out to God for relief. While I was determined to avoid being bullied out of my job, I was desperate to know what God's will was.

During this time I read Rick Warren's *The Purpose Driven Life*. The life-application questions in the book led me to discover that I loved encouraging and counseling others. These were areas of passion. I committed to spending time in prayer and fasting to hear God's heart in the matter. In the months following, I had a feeling that I would be leaving my job even though I was not actively seeking employment elsewhere. I started cleaning up my work files. I even began taking home my personal belongings. It's hard to explain why I had this feeling.

In August 2007, I decided to take a few days off of work to seek God more intently in prayer. I had a strong sense that I was to wholly devote my life to the work of the Lord by working in a faith-based environment. I couldn't bear another day of going into the office without knowing what my next steps should be.

God met me in two powerful ways, beginning one Wednesday evening at my church's prayer service. Pastor Lorna Brown, one of our elders and the wife of my senior pastor, Bishop Carlton T. Brown, spoke a prophetic word over the congregation. She said that someone present had accepted a job that this person shouldn't have accepted.

Her words pierced me. I immediately began to ask God if this word was directed at me. I spoke to Pastor Lorna after the service. When she asked how I came to obtain my job, I shared that a friend had referred me.

She looked at me in awe and said, "I did not say all that the Lord spoke as I shared the prophetic word. God also said, 'She got the job through her friend.'"

I was floored! My friend *had* helped me land the job. Pastor Lorna cautioned me to avoid making a hasty decision about leaving my job without receiving a clear confirmation of God's direction to do so.

The next day I went back to church for our noonday prayer service. Pastor Johnny Green led prayer this day. We went through the entire service and I did not hear any instruction from the Lord concerning my situation. I left church feeling discouraged. It was now Thursday, and I knew I had to return to work on the following day. As I walked to my car, I passed a senior citizen's assisted-living building. A yellow piece of paper on the ground caught my eye. It was shaped like a prism, and I could see a large, green sticker on the front. I continued walking past the paper but then asked myself, *Are you going to just walk past it?* I turned back to pick up the paper, which read, *Your faith instructions before bed tonight.* I was floored again!

The first phrase on the paper was this: "Receive this prophetic word from the Lord," followed by these verses of Scripture:

When you pass through the waters,
  I will be with you;
and when you pass through the rivers,
  they will not sweep over you.

When you walk through the fire,
  you will not be burned;
the flames will not set you ablaze. (Isaiah 43:2)

The matter was settled for me. I would resign from my job. Yet I bargained with God for a few more weeks to save money. When I shared with my parents my decision to resign, they were shocked. I didn't blame them. My decision was radical! I did not have the prospect of a new job or any savings to fall back on, and two months earlier I had enrolled in Nyack College's Alliance Graduate School of Counseling.

The next day I returned to work and was immediately called into my boss's office. Her boss was present also. She laid out for me problems with my work performance. I couldn't believe what was happening. Before I could process my thoughts, my boss gave me two options: improve my work performance in a week's time or resign!

For the third time in three days I was floored! I had gone from being a celebrated employee to one labeled as unqualified and inefficient. Yet I saw this as God's shove to move in the direction he was leading. I resigned from my job that day and left the office feeling an incredible peace. God had spoken.

I started graduate school that fall and later transferred to Alliance Theological Seminary. During that time, someone offered to pay my school tuition in full. I was so humbled and grateful that God would bless me in this way while confirming that I operated in his will.

I was unemployed for the four years I attended seminary. I graduated with distinction, receiving a Master of Professional Studies degree with a concentration in pastoral counseling. My business, Longevity Wedding Consultants, Inc., which I had started five years earlier, was not generating steady income. Since

I could barely afford the basic necessities, I had to do without cable TV and an internet hookup. My hair was falling out due to stress. I borrowed money constantly. I began to doubt whether I had clearly heard from God and made the right decision to leave my job. How could all of this hardship represent God's providence?

Have you ever asked God this question?

Despite tremendous hardship, my faith soared. I found intimacy with God. Jesus was no longer just the God I read about in the Bible; he became the God who kept me from being homeless, who fed me when I was hungry, who provided money to put gas in my car, and paid my bills. He was the God who comforted me when I would cry myself to sleep in doubt and despair. He identified generous people—family and friends—to help me financially and to encourage me emotionally when I was at my lowest points. He became my covenant keeper when he opened the door for me to receive a full-time job at a faith-based nonprofit organization called the New York City Leadership Center (now Movement.org), where I worked for eight years catalyzing Christian leaders to spiritually and socially influence their city.

I *had* heard God clearly. It *is* my life's work to be wholly devoted to serving God and his people however and wherever he sees fit. I would not be writing this book today had it not been for this radical season of faith. My convictions literally changed the course of my destiny.

That same little girl who stood up to her bullies now had to stand firm through God's leadership process as she learned to unleash the power of her voice while uncovering her purpose.

HOW WILL YOU RESPOND?

The platform God has given to me is to empower a generation of radical, emerging leaders who will take a stand for God first and then be launched by God to take a stand for others. If I had listened to the voices around me that told me I was crazy to leave MSKCC, I would have never discovered my purpose. Today, I advocate for and encourage people to be courageous in their pursuit of purpose. Whether through preaching and teaching, leading Bible study groups, or through mentoring relationships, I stand with others as they make radical, faith-filled decisions in the way that I had wanted people to stand with me when I felt defeated and vulnerable.

God often requires us to make radical decisions to prove where our allegiance lies. Are we seeking his approval or the approval of others? We may find it hard to stand for God and weather the trials that come from a decision to walk by faith and not by sight. But I am here to encourage you: don't give up and don't give in! The power of God on display in your life will demand that you be radical and unmoved in your convictions.

If we take stock of the condition of our world—deep-seated racism, the fear of the other, pervasive sexual harassment and abuse of power, an increase in human trafficking—it is evident that there is tremendous injustice all around us. But in response to those injustices there has been a growing movement to withstand those forces. This is evident in the #MeToo movement and Black Lives Matter.

I wasn't alive for the birth of the civil rights movement, but I wonder if before that movement began, the hope of possibilities filled the atmosphere, as it does today. What if now is the time to raise our voices? What if now is the time to be part of the change we desire?

People everywhere are declaring that *enough is enough!* They are taking a stand against injustice and standing with those who need support. I believe this book is a reminder that God wants to use the power of your voice to answer the cry for authentic leadership, to work with others to achieve lasting change.

In Romans 8:19 the apostle Paul writes, "The creation waits in eager expectation for the children of God to be revealed." Humanity awaits those champions of the voiceless and the powerless to reclaim victory over oppression. So, consider this question: How is God revealing his purposes through you to answer the cry of his people?

ONE MAN'S RESPONSE

In 1994, 70 percent of Africans had never heard a telephone ring. Strive Masiyiwa, founder and chairman of Econet Group, had an idea: What if his company could connect the continent of Africa by telephone? When Masiyiwa shared the vision with his staff, they balked at the idea. It was too big—it couldn't be done. So Masiyiwa reduced the immediate size of the vision and refined it to establish a viable telecommunications infrastructure in Zimbabwe.

In order to accomplish this vision, Econet had to receive approval from the government. The government, however, had its own telecommunications entity and was unwilling to empower Econet to develop a new system. This led to a five-year legal battle against the government. At times Masiyiwa felt defeated and questioned whether or not he had made the right decision. But he believed in God's power to overcome this obstacle. Consequently, God sent people to encourage him on the journey.

Employees of Econet describe Masiyiwa as a man of unwavering faith. He will not embark upon a new idea without first bending his knees in prayer.

Masiyiwa and Econet won their legal battle and acquired the telephone license from the government. Today, Econet is Zimbabwe's largest telecommunications firm with a subscriber base of well over thirteen million and growing. Masiyiwa also became Zimbabwe's first billionaire!

Our God is a God of victory. He simply requires a willing person to lead. Masiyiwa dared to believe that the vision inside of him reflected the heart of God.

YOUR LEADERSHIP JOURNEY

Leaders like Masiyiwa infuse others with a vision beyond their current horizon. Who is that kind of leader? When we keep at the forefront of our mind that God is the creator of all we are and is helping us do what he has called us to do, this posture of gratitude to the one who has redeemed us and cemented our identity will infuse all that we accomplish.

We can't lead others without vision. A major aspect of effective leadership is helping people move from one place to another. We have to be able to cast the vision of where we're going, how we will get there, and the role each person must play to accomplish the goal. People will follow us when we've demonstrated relational trust in the past, even if they can't clearly see where we're headed.

Perhaps you too have found yourself thrust into surprising places of leadership. Or you might be looking for a fresh start in your approach to life and leadership. Every part of your life— good, bad, or indifferent—is a distinct marker God uses to hardwire you for purpose. That's the theme of the first part of this book—how God shapes us as leaders through his power and presence.

The power of God's presence is not just for our benefit but for all in our sphere of influence. It's quite amazing how our obedience to God unleashes a ripple effect that can alter the destiny of generations to come. Thus, the second part of this book is an exploration of the leadership skills we develop and the contexts where we will use them.

At the end of each chapter are some reflection questions. You may find it helpful to journal through them on your own and to bring them into a conversation with a mentor. They also provide great material for small group discussions. You might want to work through them as you read each chapter or come back to them later or not use them at all! Feel free to use them in the way and in the timing that best serves your needs.

Masiyiwa reminds me of Queen Esther. When confronted with the news of the imminent destruction of her people, she was faced with a decision: choose the comfort of her position as queen and remain silent or use the power of her position to advocate for those being oppressed. At a critical moment when the lives of her people, the Jews, hung in the balance, God used another leader, her uncle Mordecai, to speak into her life. Mordecai said, "If you remain silent at this time, relief and deliverance for the Jews will arise from another place, but you and your father's family will perish. And who knows but that you have come to your royal position for such a time as this?" (Esther 4:14).

God had already positioned Esther to respond to the need. Yet Esther had to embark upon a process of prayer and fasting to uncover her own willingness to respond to that need. For the present-day battles we face, I simply ask this question: Are you the one, or should we look for another?

God will train us to recognize the truths he's been speaking to us all along. This book will encourage us to recognize the needs of those around us and to find God's purpose in difficult situations.

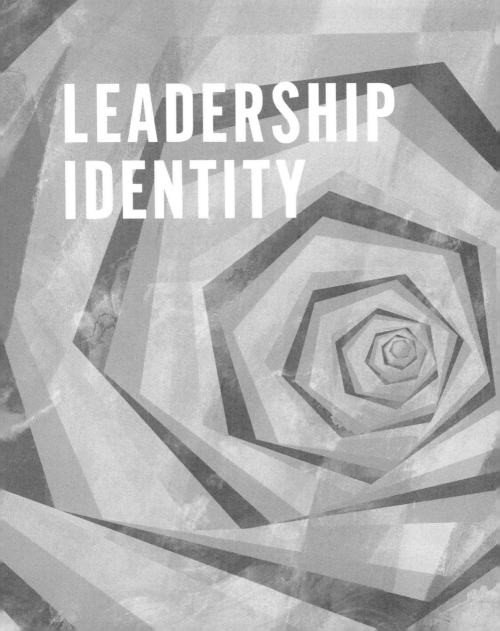

PART ONE

LEADERSHIP IDENTITY

CHAPTER ONE

THE POWER OF GOD'S PRESENCE

Moses said to the LORD, "You have been telling me, 'Lead these people,' but you have not let me know whom you will send with me." . . .
The LORD replied, "My Presence will go with you, and I will give you rest."

EXODUS 33:12-14

ON A TUESDAY EVENING in April 2012, I was in the middle of my weekly thirty-minute prayer call with a friend Ifeytaya Bulow-Deck. There I was, sitting in the foyer of my parents' home with my eyes closed when, suddenly, images of the men in my family marched through my mind one after the other. My father. My uncles. My brother. My cousins. With them came an over-whelming sense that someone was about to die.

I panicked. Was one of them *dying*? Why was I having these thoughts? While I thought about what to do next, I prayed for my father, uncles, brother, and cousins. Soon, I sensed the Holy Spirit leading me to declare Psalm 118:17: "[They] shall not die but live, and declare the works of the LORD" (KJV). I prayed those words repeatedly. At that moment it was all I could do. The intensity of my prayer took on a form of its own as God led me to confidently pray the Word with authority and conviction. All the while my mind raced to understand what was seemingly a supernatural God encounter.

Ifeytaya was supportive as always during our prayer times. She prayed in agreement with me that these men would not die but live. She also expressed her belief that God would protect my family.

I got off the phone with Ifeytaya puzzled and concerned yet trusting that God had revealed what the enemy had intended. What was intended for evil, however, would be turned around for our good (Genesis 50:20). I wanted to tell someone but didn't want to alarm anyone. Instead, I prayed daily for the protection of the men in my family.

In May, my mom told our family that my uncle Tony (her brother) had been diagnosed four months earlier with stage 4 colon cancer and had only just shared this news after she asked him why he was in the bed all of the time. He was fifty-three years old.

I was shocked. Mad at him too. Why had he held this information for so long? Why was he resigned to die? We could have done something! Also troubling was the fact that I wasn't sure whether he had a personal relationship with God.

It was then that I remembered my prayer to the Lord the month before. *My uncle was the one I'd needed to pray for!*

My mom convinced Uncle Tony to allow her to make a doctor's appointment for him at Mt. Sinai Hospital in New York City for a second opinion. As Mom and I stood in the oncology department waiting room at Mt. Sinai waiting for the doctor to return with his report, I scanned the room trying to process the desperation and despair on so many faces. How did we get here? What would my family have to endure?

The doctor returned and said the cancer was indeed stage 4.

"How much time does he have to live?" I asked, a question I dreaded.

"Six months," the doctor replied.

Six months! This can't be real! I panicked, tears flowing. Meanwhile, my mom remained calm and continued to ask wise questions about how we could care for my uncle. She didn't accept the timetable of death.

As thoughts of my uncle's life, his children, and the rest of our family flooded my mind, the Holy Spirit reminded me that God alone determines when we live and die. So I prayed again, *Lord, please spare my uncle's life. Don't take him from this earth until I have the assurance that he'll be with you in heaven.*

Uncle Tony received chemotherapy but continued to deteriorate. I felt so powerless against this disease. Though I was a minister in training, someone who was supposed to lead others, I was overwhelmed.

One Sunday after church at the home my uncle and grandmother shared, I looked at my uncle, now very gaunt and withdrawn, and I burst into tears. How full of life he used to be.

"It's going to be okay," Uncle Tony said.

But I knew that wasn't true. This was not okay.

Watching Uncle Tony die was one of the hardest things I've ever faced. It was even more devastating knowing that he didn't want to die and hadn't made peace with his condition.

We decided that Uncle Tony would receive hospice care in his home. But he needed more support than we could provide. Since he was too fragile to be moved, we asked God for grace and strength. We knew it was only a matter of time before he would pass away. He was barely talking and had stopped eating.

Feeling desperate and unsure whether or not Uncle Tony had ever talked to God about forgiveness, I asked my mentor, Helen

West, one of the elders at my church—Bethel Gospel Assembly—to come and pray for Uncle Tony. I *needed* to know that he would be with the Lord after he died.

My uncle lay there as Elder West entered the room. I watched and silently prayed that God would show his presence. Elder West talked to him and read to him passages from the Bible. After that, she asked him if he wanted to have a relationship with God, to acknowledge that the wrongs my uncle had committed had been dealt with when Jesus died on the cross. Because of that, he could have peace with God. If he understood that, he was to raise his hand.

I studied Uncle Tony intently for any sign of movement.

Nothing.

Had he heard her? Would God answer my prayer?

I prayed again. Slowly, his right hand moved, lifting off the bed. He'd heard! He wanted to be at peace with God.

Four days later my uncle took his final breath. But I knew that death was not the final answer for him. He would be with the Lord for eternity. The joy and release that I felt were indescribable.

Elder West gave the eulogy at my uncle's homegoing service. We chose to call the service a "homegoing" instead of a funeral because we believed that he indeed went home to his final resting place in heaven with the Lord (2 Corinthians 5:8).

I couldn't help recalling my prayer for the men in my family back in April. God had answered by showing the power of his presence during one of the most difficult times my family had faced.

Have you ever felt out of your depth as a leader? Another man felt way out of his league when handed an assignment. His name was Moses.

MOSES MAKES A PLAN: TAKE ONE

Moses' familiar story has been the subject of films—*Exodus: Gods and Kings* (2014), *The Ten Commandments* (1956)—and novels such as *Moses, Man of the Mountain* by Zora Neale Hurston. It began with a problem that needed a solution.

For centuries the Israelites—who were then known as the Hebrews—were slaves in Egypt. Slavery was Pharaoh's chosen means of population control (Exodus 3:8-14). Their cries of anguish had reached God (Exodus 3:7-9), and he decided "to rescue them from the hand of the Egyptians and to bring them up out of that land into a good and spacious land, a land flowing with milk and honey" (Exodus 3:8). But he would use a man to do it.

Moses was an unlikely choice for a deliverer—the kind of story Hollywood loves. He was born to Amram and Jochebed (Numbers 26:58-59) at the worst time for male babies to be born. Having survived Pharaoh's second method of population control—killing male Hebrew babies (Exodus 1:15-22)—he had been raised by the current Pharaoh's daughter (Exodus 2:1-10). So far so good. But around the age of forty, Moses witnessed an Egyptian's cruelty to one of his own people. Driven by concern for the oppression of his people, Moses saw this as his call to action. So, he murdered the man and quickly buried him (Exodus 2:11-12).

Not the ideal resume entry for the job of deliverer.

Moses had been seen and was forced to flee to Midian to escape Pharaoh's demand for justice (Exodus 2:13–15). He'd blown it.

MOSES MAKES A PLAN: TAKE TWO

You've heard stories of celebrities who were downgraded from fame and fortune to anonymity and sometimes poverty. Moses, the celebrity of his day, had gone from being the adopted son of the daughter of Pharaoh to being a nobody in the wilderness with nothing but the clothes on his back. But there was a silver cloud on the horizon. After helping a group of shepherdesses (Exodus 2:16-17), he gained a wife, a new home, and a new responsibility: being a shepherd over the flock of his father-in-law, Jethro.

Despite Moses' failed attempt and forced retreat, God still had plans for Moses. Forty years of seasoning as a husband to Zipporah and a shepherd in the wilderness of Midian had rendered Moses ready to lead. But in Exodus 3, Moses encountered God's presence in a unique way

In *The Hero with a Thousand Faces*, Joseph Campbell's seminal work on the hero's journey, one of the steps of the hero's journey is the call to action. Moses' call to action was literally God calling to him from a burning bush: "And now the cry of the Israelites has reached me, and I have seen the way the Egyptians are oppressing them. So now, go. I am sending you to Pharaoh to bring my people the Israelites out of Egypt" (Exodus 3:9-10).

Imagine how you would feel if you heard the voice of God calling to you from a tree or a bush outside your home and giving you an assignment. What would you say first? Do first?

Keep in mind that Moses had never heard the voice of God. He wasn't exactly sure who was speaking to him. As Exodus 3:13 describes it: "Then Moses said to God, 'If I come to the people of Israel and say to them, "The God of your fathers has sent me to you," and they ask me, "What is his name?" what shall I say to them?'" (ESV). Sounds like a stalling technique, doesn't it?

Moses felt completely unqualified and lamented to God that he was a man of lowly position. Look at his list of excuses in Exodus 4. How could he be the best for this assignment?

The Leader in You Chart

Moses' Excuse (Exodus 4)	God's Response
What if they do not believe me or listen to me and say, "The LORD did not appear to you"? (v. 1)	What is that in your hand?... Throw [the staff] on the ground.... This is so that they may believe that the LORD, the God of their fathers—the God of Abraham, the God of Isaac and the God of Jacob—has appeared to you. (vv. 2-5)
I have never been eloquent, neither in the past nor since you have spoken to your servant. I am slow of speech and tongue. (v. 10)	Who gave human beings their mouths? Who makes them deaf or mute? Who gives them sight or makes them blind? Is it not I, the LORD? Now go; I will help you speak and will teach you what to say. (vv. 11-12)
Please send someone else. (v. 13)	What about your brother, Aaron the Levite?.... You shall speak to him and put words in his mouth; I will help both of you speak and will teach you what to do. (vv. 14-15)

With every doubt Moses had about his ability to lead, God responded by showing Moses that he had already made provision for his journey—the provision of the Lord himself.

God showed Moses and us that he equips us with everything we need to effectively lead. Resources are already at our disposal, often already within us. We come to understand how the presence of God can be found in the promises throughout the Bible, the language of prayer, hearing the voice of God within our spirit, and also through those who provide wise counsel.

MY BURNING BUSH

I can relate to Moses' feelings of inadequacy. In 2001, after I graduated from the State University of New York at Binghamton, I moved back to the Bronx, where my family lived. It was a hard adjustment. I was no longer closely connected to my community of friends. I had become a working professional and resumed an on-again-off-again relationship with a guy I'll call Scott.

I met Scott when I was seventeen, a few months before I left for Binghamton. He had graduated from college a few months prior and was in car sales. He had some of the qualities I wanted in a man: handsome, stylish, confident.

Back then, I had so many unresolved issues from the absence of a relationship with my dad. I felt like a ship lost at sea with no sense of direction. I yearned for love and affirmation.

But I really didn't know what to look for in a boyfriend. Though I wasn't looking for marriage, I wanted the consistency of a relationship with someone I could be comfortable with.

A week after meeting Scott it became painfully clear that he was self-absorbed and in no way was looking to be in a committed relationship with me. Still, I continued to see him from time to time until I left for school. Over my four years at Binghamton I would contact him periodically with the hopes that there would have been some change in his posture toward me. On every phone call he was abrupt. He never asked questions about how I was doing, how was school, and the like.

After graduating, I went back to dating Scott. We only spent time together when he was available—no matter the time of day or night. I was so starved for companionship that I accepted whatever behavior was dished out despite how deeply those actions wounded me. I didn't value myself enough to demand better treatment even if doing so resulted in him no longer being in my life.

I'm ashamed to say how long I was in this relationship. We were in an on-again-off-again state for ten years. Where's the SMH (shaking my head/face-palm) emoji when you need one?

Finally, things came to a head in 2003 when Scott tried to convince me to (1) have a child with him and (2) accept that he would always be romantically involved with other women. Mind you, we were not yet in a committed relationship. And the crazy thing is I actually entertained his proposition, thinking perhaps this was as good as it would get for me. I had grown to love Scott. We had fun times together. But it was time to let Scott go.

I was hurting, lonely, and unsure of who I was. Throughout my academic career I had been a scholar, receiving countless awards. I had studied abroad in Paris and Voronezh, Russia. For three summers during high school, I had had a phenomenal internship at the New York Mercantile Exchange through Jobs for Youth, sponsored by Pfizer. Much of my identity was tied to my accomplishments. But after graduation the silence of my present life left me feeling empty.

As I was sitting in my bedroom one afternoon, I decided to read my Bible—something I rarely did. I opened to Matthew 15:8-9:

These people honor me with their lips,
    but their hearts are far from me.
They worship me in vain;
    their teachings are merely human rules.

Tears streamed down my face as the words echoed within me. This was my "burning bush"—God reaching out to me through the Bible. Somehow, I knew that God was describing my spiritual condition as being *far from him*. My priorities in life were all about what I wanted or what Scott wanted. A relationship with God was nowhere on my radar. Other than a quick prayer before I ate, for protection before I traveled, or when I needed a job after graduating from college, there was no intimacy with God. I didn't desire it or see examples around me that would demonstrate that an intimate relationship with God was possible. My life was work, partying with friends, shopping, and dating. But at that moment, when confronted with that verse, I didn't want my heart to remain far from God. I asked God that day to draw my heart closer to his.

Months later, I wrestled with what that prayer would require of me. Though I knew that going to church was the first step toward this prayer becoming a reality, getting there was a continual battle. My social life was my priority. The allure of the clubs on Saturday night was far too exciting. Yet on Sundays I always felt defeated, like I'd made a promise to someone and hadn't kept it.

I bargained with God: if he gave me a car, I would go to church. Back then I lived in a two-fare zone, which meant I had to take a bus to the train station. On the weekends, public transportation ran at a snail's pace. I eventually bought a car but reneged on my promise to go to church.

Two years later I began attending Sunday worship services at Bethel Gospel Assembly, the church where I had first come to know Christ as a child. It was the only church I knew and the only church we attended as a family.

One Sunday the senior pastor (and later a spiritual father and mentor), Bishop Carlton T. Brown, had just finished preaching and had invited anyone in the congregation who needed prayer for a fresh start with God to come to the altar. I knew that invitation was for me. I was so tired of hurting, so tired of the lack of direction in my life.

I told God, "I've tried it my way. Your way has got to be better." That was the moment I became willing to live on God's terms—his way, his will be done, not my way or my will.

During this time, I found the strength to completely sever my relationship and end all communication with Scott. We were parked outside of my parents' house in his car. Since I cared for him, I took the time to explain to him what God had done in my life and the life I now desired to live for God. But he didn't understand. In a moment of sincerity, he asked me if I thought he was the devil. Sensing how fragile he was, I tried to offer reassurance while speaking the truth in love (Ephesians 4:15). Because he had not given his life to the Lord, he would be a hindrance to what God wanted to do in my life.

I still can't believe the strength I exhibited during those moments. For many years afterward I prayed for Scott. I still do. I desperately want God to save his soul.

On December 31, 2005, I attended what we call the Watch Night Service—the yearly New Year's Eve worship service. The tradition at the church was for each person to receive a "faith promise"—a prophetic word from passages of Scripture, which was considered to be a word from God for the year. Receiving this promise was a highlight of the service. I picked out of the bowl a card with two verses:

> Consequently, you are no longer foreigners and strangers, but fellow citizens with God's people and also members of his household. (Ephesians 2:19)

> The LORD replied, "My Presence will go with you, and I will give you rest." (Exodus 33:14)

I smiled from ear to ear as I walked back to the pew. God had heard my prayer two years earlier and had been working in me to complete the good work he had begun in my life. My joy was indescribable. But I couldn't help wondering what was next.

HIS PRESENCE ALONG MY PATH

God sent me back to Bethel Gospel Assembly in New York City, the church where I first acknowledged that Jesus was my Lord and Savior at the age of eleven. There I joined the women's ministry, Alabaster Women of Faith, under the leadership of Rev. Wendie Gail Howlett-Trott.

Wendie was the first woman ordained as an elder at Bethel in the mid-1990s. She was and still is a trailblazer. When I enrolled in Nyack College's Alliance Theological Seminary and had to identify a mentor, she was my first choice. She graciously accepted and immediately asked me to develop a curriculum for a women's empowerment group. I was honored to do so and put forth my best effort at a curriculum that I thought would serve *her* well as she led the group. What I didn't know was that she would give me the assignment of leadership.

When the leadership was offered, I was dumbfounded and felt completely unqualified. Have you ever felt that way? I didn't grow up going to church every Sunday. I was a "CME" Christian: someone who went to church for special occasions—Christmas, Mother's Day, and Easter! I was also twenty-nine years old! How could I lead women older than me, let alone my peers?

As I wrestled with all that I was being asked to do, I remembered what God said in Exodus 33:14. He would go with me and give me rest. So I accepted and wound up leading that ministry for five years. Hundreds of women from our church and the community took part in the Bible studies we offered.

I received my first preaching assignment to minister at a local Harlem church by way of a woman who attended an empowerment group. Empowerment was a group of thirty to forty women who were then divided into smaller groups of five or six, each with a small group facilitator. While I was the overall leader, our facilitators would colead a weekly study, focusing on discussion questions to unpack the ways God wanted to empower us. I can't help wondering: If I had not responded to God's invitation to a deeper relationship with him in 2003 where might I and all of these other women be today?

Those five years were a time for training, preparation, and instruction. The opportunity to lead the ministry launched me into a greater place of service and devotion to God. I would later be ordained and become one of the youngest elders of our church.

When we're in need of a fresh start, it can be easy to downgrade our past as memories to forget instead of blocks to build on.

Every measure of our life—good, bad, or indifferent—is a distinct marker that God uses to hardwire us for purpose.

The power of God's presence is not just for our benefit but for all in our sphere of influence. It's quite amazing how our obedience to God unleashes a ripple effect that can alter the destiny of generations to come.

REFLECTION QUESTIONS

1. When was the last time you felt inadequate? What did you do as a result?

2. When did you first recognize your need for God? What happened after that?

3. What opportunities have you had to lead others?

4. What are you passionate about?

5. Who would you help if you could? Why?

6. What resources has God given you as a leader?

7. What skills do you have to offer?

CHAPTER TWO

DISCERNING THE TIMES AND SEASONS

I said to them, "You see the trouble we are in:
Jerusalem lies in ruins, and its gates have been burned with
fire. Come, let us rebuild the wall of Jerusalem,
and we will no longer be in disgrace." . . .
So they began this good work.

NEHEMIAH 2:17-18

IN OCTOBER 2018, I attended the annual gathering of the Table Coalition (TTC), where I serve on the board. The Table Coalition grew out of the US Lausanne Committee for World Evangelization and partners with the church in America to help introduce Jesus to people from all walks of life. There I met John Perkins, a teacher I had long respected.

At the age of eighty-eight John is a vivacious pioneer for social justice and a fountain of wisdom, strength, courage, and conviction. At TTC, John shared topics from his latest book, *One Blood*, which he describes as his "final manifesto." In the book he writes, "Issues of justice, diversity, and reconciliation are not extra add-ons that the church can opt out of as a matter of personal preference. They are an essential part of the gospel." Where today's news stories and social media platforms broadcast these issues for our awareness and action, Perkins reminds us that the church bears a responsibility to respond as a prophetic voice taking a stand against injustice.

John was born in 1930 in New Hebron, Mississippi, during the pinnacle of racial segregation. He dropped out of school in the third grade. After his brother Clyde was murdered by a white police officer, John moved to California out of fear that he would meet a similar fate.

In California he developed a firm understanding of capitalism and understood that whoever controlled the capital controlled the environment. It was here also that he became a Christian at the age of twenty-seven through the testimony of his son.

In 1960, John made the decision to return to Mendenhall, Mississippi, after many visits to children's prisons in California. He saw himself and his environment through the lives of these youths. As he listened to their stories, he knew that many had come from the South. He wanted to go back and serve his people, rescuing them from the injustice of mental and physical oppression.

After returning to Mendenhall, John began to rally those around him to protest against racial injustice. As a consequence he was beaten and jailed many times. During one protest he was arrested and tortured in jail in an attempt to stop him and others from protesting. In a video John explains that during that time of torment in prison, "I saw the absolute necessity for reconciliation. I saw the depths of racism."

While recovering in the hospital and being cared for by white doctors and nurses, John came to terms with the hatred he had developed toward white people because of the brutality he had suffered. Though he wanted to hate them, love won out. With that knowledge the need for reconciliation grew. He promised God that if he survived the experience, he would preach a gospel that would destroy some of the hate he had experienced. Blacks and whites could heal each other.

Perkins's life has revolutionized a generation to actualize the power of the gospel to transform not just individual lives but whole communities. He followed the legacy of many courageous leaders before him, those who discerned what was needed to bring about change in the world.

The story of one such leader can be found in the Old Testament. His name is Nehemiah.

TOO MUCH IS AT STAKE

The heart of Nehemiah was gripped by the condition of Jerusalem, a city with a tumultuous history.

Here's a little back story. After the death of King Solomon, the twelve tribes of Israel were divided into two kingdoms: the southern kingdom, which had two tribes—Judah and Benjamin—under the command of King Rehoboam (son of King Solomon), and the northern kingdom, which included the remaining ten tribes led by Jeroboam, a former servant of King Solomon. God had made a covenant with Israel as his chosen people. In Deuteronomy 28, God spoke through Moses about the blessings and curses associated with obedience or disobedience. Some of these curses involved an enemy nation that would swoop in, besiege the nation, eat the crops of the land, and carry off the people (Deuteronomy 28:39-64).

After centuries of disobedience, Israel experienced the fulfillment of these curses. God allowed the northern kingdom to be taken captive by the Assyrians, and 150 years later God allowed the nation of Judah to be taken captive by the Babylonians. After seventy years in Babylonian exile, many Jews were allowed to return to Judah and rebuild the city of Jerusalem and repair the temple.

Ezra the priest was sent back to Jerusalem to teach the people about the law of Moses. But the wall around the city, which had been destroyed by the invading army of Nebuchadnezzar (2 Kings 25), had never been rebuilt.

During this return to Judah, Nehemiah's brother, Hanani, and a few other men reported that those who had returned from exile were in great distress. Nehemiah was a cupbearer to the king of Persia. Upon hearing about the condition of his people and the city (Nehemiah 1:1-3), he could have shown apathy. After all, he didn't live in Jerusalem. The people had received their just punishment for disobeying God. Instead, Nehemiah chose to respond with empathy, which involved repentance, weeping, fasting, and prayer for the forgiveness and restoration of his people. While praying, Nehemiah sought favor with God to go before the king and request to be sent to Judah. God granted his request.

Nehemiah arrived at Jerusalem and stayed there three days before gathering some men to inspect the city by night. After they toured the broken walls, Nehemiah revealed what was in his heart for Jerusalem: "You see the bad situation that we are in— how Jerusalem is desolate *and* lies in ruins and its gates have been burned with fire. Come, and let us rebuild the wall of Jerusalem, so that we will no longer be a disgrace" (Nehemiah 2:17 Amplified). The people responded that they would rise up and build.

The builders immediately faced opposition from Sanballat the Horonite, Tobiah the Ammonite, and Geshem the Arab (Nehemiah 6:1). Each was a regional governor serving under the king of Persia. Sanballat and Tobiah represented two groups that God had driven out of the Promised Land to give to the Israelites. Some of Israel's enemies had returned to the Promised Land and had a vested interest in seeing Jerusalem remain in ruins. These three men represented the enemies of God.

Though Sanballat, Tobiah, and Geshem did not relent in their intimidation of the workers, Nehemiah's response to these men was rooted in the same determination to persevere past distractions and intimidation. He encouraged the workers to avoid giving into fear, because God was with them.

Consider a time when you felt intimidated by opposition. Perhaps you're facing such a time right now. Let Nehemiah's response be your guide. The work you are doing is too great to be distracted to a point of inefficiency. Too much is at stake to give in to intimidation.

Many leaders in history understood this firsthand. Let me tell you about one of them: Thurgood Marshall.

BREAKING THROUGH THE WALL

Like John Perkins, Thurgood Marshall grew up in the years when Jim Crow laws were enforced and segregation was a way of life. Not everyone agreed with that standard, however. Many saw it as a wall keeping certain people in and others out.

Thurgood Marshall was born in 1908 in Baltimore and later attended Lincoln University in Pennsylvania. At Lincoln, Marshall began his career as a civil rights crusader when he joined his friends to desegregate the all-white section of a movie theater. He wanted to attend the University of Maryland Law School but didn't apply, fearing he would not be permitted entry due to race. Instead, he applied to and was accepted by Howard University Law School in Washington, DC.

During his time at Howard, Marshall was mentored by Charles Hamilton Houston, the dean of the law school. Hamilton taught Marshall how to use litigation to undermine social injustice and bring about social reform. In 1951, with the support of the National Association for the Advancement of Colored People (NAACP), a landmark case was filed in Topeka, Kansas. When

Oliver Brown's daughter Linda was refused enrollment in any of the all-white elementary schools, he took legal action. While the US District of Kansas agreed with Brown about the unequal education system, the court did not challenge the "separate but equal" doctrine. Separate but equal meant that despite segregation, under the guise of the law, persons of different racial and ethnic backgrounds were still considered to be equal although it was evident from the unequal education system equality was not be actualized in communities of color. The next year the US Supreme Court combined the case of Mr. Brown with four others under one name: *Brown v. Board of Education of Topeka*. The lead attorney for the plaintiffs in this case was Thurgood Marshall, who presided over the NAACP Legal Defense and Education Fund.

Marshall understood that courage was needed for such an undertaking as *Brown v. Board of Education of Topeka*. He risked his life time and time again to argue cases of injustice in the court of law. As a result, he received many death threats. None of those stopped him. He made America think about the injustices that had become a daily way of life, and he brilliantly gained equality through the law.

On May 17, 1954, the Supreme Court ruled against the segregation of schools, deciding unanimously that the plaintiffs had been deprived of equal protection under the laws guaranteed by the Fourteenth Amendment. District courts and school boards were ordered to desegregate the schools. Yet this was hindered in many places.

Thurgood Marshall argued thirty-two cases before the Supreme Court, winning twenty-nine of them—the most in US history. He became the first African American appointed as an associate justice of the US Supreme Court. His conviction and determination to stand against injustice repaired many broken walls within our justice system.

AN AWAKENING

We all have areas of passion that God stirs within us, areas that lead to transformation in our and others' lives. I liken this stirring to God-ordained trigger points that are catalytic in nature.

I am passionate about service, imparting wisdom, seeing injustice and oppression combatted, and developing emerging leaders. As a young person growing up in Spanish Harlem (New York City), when I learned that my female neighbors were victims of domestic violence, I didn't ignore their cries for help. I called 911 and hoped that my neighbors would press charges against their abusers or seek safety elsewhere. I couldn't close my ears to the pain and pretend I hadn't heard. God hadn't wired me that way. I'd rather act than regret.

In 2015, Rev. Dr. Brenda Salter McNeil, another social justice champion, gave a talk at Movement Day, a gathering for Christian leaders who want to spiritually and socially transform their cities. She said, "Our silence is violence." If we don't respond who will?

Some people stop to help those in trouble while others walk way. They run toward danger rather than away from it because they bear a sense of responsibility and hope that they can be used by God to change this situation. We too can respond this way, because we view life through the lens of hope and possibilities. Faith in God is the key to our ability to see miracles of transformation occur.

Through this lens of hope we are not dismayed by what we see. And even in times of discouragement, we can be renewed in the promise of God's Word.

Reverend Dr. Mac Pier, the founder of Movement.org (formerly the New York City Leadership Center), my place of employment for eight years, has said at many Movement Day gatherings, "What God wants to do in a city, he has already put in the hearts of its leaders."

LEADING AT THE TACTICAL LEVEL

In every professional role I've had since college, I've had the freedom to chart my own path while developing a benchmark for success going forward. Being entrusted with responsibility is exhilarating. I'm an analytical thinker. I thrive when given administrative tasks such as establishing order, cultivating strategic plans, building teams, and executing the ideas of visionary leaders. Having come to understand that God has gifted me in this area, I'm usually able to pinpoint what my involvement might be when new opportunities come my way. Though God could call me to a different arena and equip me to accept different responsibilities, my past experience has served as a great indicator of the types of assignments God might lead me to accept.

In 2016, I was given the assignment to lead a team of seasoned leaders with a local New York City organization. The idea excited me. We would develop programming to confront issues of prejudice and injustice within the community. I didn't realize we'd have to first confront opposition within the team.

Based on conversations and the actions of some of the team members, I could tell that they didn't want me to lead. Instead, they wanted me to be onboard with *their* vision. My directives were questioned, and there was a constant resistance to the establishment of order in our planning processes, which would have brought clarity to the entire team.

I didn't realize what was happening at first, but subconsciously I started justifying my experience and the knowledge that qualified me to have a seat at the table. It would take me a few weeks to realize that I did this because I sensed that my leadership was being challenged. An us-versus-them mentality also emerged as we worked with community partners. We needed to work with these groups and could not afford to alienate them, no matter how ineffective we felt their policies might be. The spirit and culture of the team, often revealed through an elitist viewpoint, ran counter to my leadership style, my character, and my integrity. I felt that I had stepped into a minefield and needed to quickly learn new tools of engagement to navigate it.

I had been leading teams for nine years prior to this new assignment. Yet within a few weeks I doubted my ability to effectively lead this group. I always pray before saying yes to any new assignment. But in this case I thought perhaps I hadn't heard God clearly. Maybe I accepted this assignment to please people rather than God.

But then I remembered to get back to basics. Like Nehemiah, I fasted and prayed to the God of heaven. I needed God to

- reveal what might be hidden from my understanding of how to effectively lead and serve this team.

- free me from a mindset that might hinder our advancement.

- reveal any inadequacies in my leadership and equip me with the tools to reengage this group and bring forth the unity necessary to serve our community.

Through the wise counsel of my mentors I was reminded to pray strategically as I reflected on Scriptures that would help me lead in the face of opposition.

It's hard to be disliked, talked about, or falsely accused. Though I wanted to quit, I knew a bigger picture had yet to be revealed. I needed to rise above my emotions and remind myself that I had the mind of Christ, as Paul stated in 1 Corinthians 2:16.

I remained with the team of seasoned leaders. Within three months we had made incredible inroads in serving the community and were able to repair some strained relationships. Since then, opportunities emerged for me to mentor members of the team. Time will continue to tell the breadth and depth of our success together.

Nehemiah's example (and the examples of other leaders in this chapter) proves that people need leaders who can help them see a way out of their present circumstance, leaders who will walk in the trenches with them and empower them to actualize change.

ARE YOU THE ONE?

In a polarized political climate, which has led to increased racial tensions, unhelpful rhetoric from our nation's leaders, and deepening discord along racial, ethnic, and socioeconomic lines, we can detect the need for authentic leadership. But those who follow Christ want to lead in ways that are anchored in God's truth and righteousness—to be peacemakers and not peacefakers.

In Matthew 11, John the Baptist was facing imminent execution. He had fulfilled his assignment—preaching the message of repentance and preparing the way for the salvation of the Lord—but in a moment of despair, he yearned for reassurance that the Messiah had indeed come. In Matthew 11:3-5, John asks Jesus,

> "Are you the one who is to come, or should we expect someone else?"
>
> Jesus replied, "Go back and report to John what you hear and see: The blind receive sight, the lame walk, those who have leprosy are cleansed, the deaf hear, the dead are raised, and the good news is proclaimed to the poor."

Today, in moments of despair—the devastation of mass shootings, the mass incarceration of people of color, the sexual harassment of women and men, human trafficking and sexual exploitation—people, like John, are asking leaders, "Are you the one who is to come, or should we expect someone else? Are you the one to promote justice, to restore peace, to bring forth restoration and healing to our communities? Are you a leader who will discern the times and seasons and determine to convey the heart of God in every matter?"

The 2016 US presidential election exposed the racial discord in America. At Movement Day 2015, while discussing ways to bridge racial divisions in communities, Rev. Bryan L. Carter, senior pastor of Concord Church in Dallas, said, "My blackness doesn't trump my Jesus-ness." In other words, we must get to a redemptive place in our spiritual identity where neither our skin color nor our politics trump our call to righteousness as Christians. We must contend for healing, restoration, and the presence of God to go with us into every assignment and give us rest.

The apostle Paul writes, "All creation is waiting eagerly for that future day when God will reveal who his children really are" (Romans 8:19 NLT). Paul was speaking not only about an eternal revelation for the believer but also a present-day truth we must wrestle with—the responsibility of the believer to rise up and be part of the change we desire to see across the spheres of influence God has given us.

REFLECTION QUESTIONS

1. Have you noticed a common theme in the type of vocational roles you've held?

2. What steps will you take to confront the opposition you will face as a leader?

3. Where do you sense God calling you to speak against injustice?

4. Has adversity caused you to doubt whether you're qualified to fulfill a certain leadership role? If so, how have you addressed this? If not, what will you do to address it?

5. How does your faith inform your politics?

CHAPTER THREE

DEVELOPING YOUR LEADERSHIP IDENTITY

*It is not the critic who counts; not the man who points
out how the strong man stumbles, or where the doer of
deeds could have done them better. The credit belongs
to the man who is actually in the arena, whose face is
marred by dust and sweat and blood; who strives valiantly;
who errs, who comes short again and again, because
there is no effort without error and shortcoming.*

THEODORE ROOSEVELT, "THE MAN IN THE ARENA"

WHEN WE WERE BORN INTO THIS WORLD, we were given
markers that spoke to our identity: name, family origin, ethnicity.
As we progress through the stages of life, each stage reveals more
of who we are. There are life-defining experiences in every stage—
traumas or triumphs—and other influences like family lineage,
the environment, and culture that shape our perceptions of self
and the way we view the world.

There comes a time when we grab ahold of the reins of our lives
and begin to wrestle with who we really are. During that time in
our lives, we intentionally reflect on our likes and dislikes and
decide our goals, values, dreams, and aspirations.

We learn to formulate opinions on all manner of issues and erect beliefs that become the foundation for how we live. Here we come to trust God's will for our lives and submit to a process of aligning our will with his. The desire to submit to God's will is a choice, one that we can only make after first being drawn to God by the Holy Spirit. This is a supernatural, life-altering process. As we wrestle with how God's Spirit makes us unique, we glimpse how God intends to use us in the world.

Our personal identity shapes our leadership identity. The two are intrinsically aligned because we lead out of the product of our experiences. This is why the development of self-perception is so critical to our ability to effectively and authentically lead others from a place of truth and power.

We need to understand ourselves and our place in the world. Our leadership journey is filled with times of introspection coupled with mentorship and the investment of more senior leaders in our lives. Learning how to make wise decisions, how to lead from a place of courage and conviction by way of challenging situations and circumstances, all become defining markers that shape us as credible life-tested leaders.

God's Word can help in this process. One of my favorite Scriptures is 2 Corinthians 4:7, "We have this treasure in jars of clay to show that this all-surpassing power is from God and not from us." Treasure is always hidden. It has to be mined and uncovered. How we choose to understand our identity reveals the hidden treasure within us that demonstrates the all-surpassing power of God on display in us.

ENDURING HARDSHIP

How leaders respond to hardship is one of the most defining markers of the leadership process. I've learned, while kicking and screaming, to accept that disappointment, failure, and pain are givens. But how we condition our minds *before* these inevitable life experiences occur will dictate their outcome.

Which brings me back to this chapter's epigraph. Teddy Roosevelt's speech "The Man in the Arena" inspires me to be strong and courageous and to honor the process attributed to the arena of life I'm presently striving to lead. Whether I succeed or fail, I can be encouraged that I am indeed in the arena by choice, not just spectating and criticizing those serving sacrificially.

Turning to another arena, I am a huge National Football League fan. In sports, football is my first love, followed by basketball. The game was introduced to me by my stepfather when I was ten. I remember watching my first Super Bowl with him on television—Super Bowl XXIV on January 28, 1990, when the San Francisco 49ers defeated the Denver Broncos. I was hooked! I marveled at the game and the incredible athletes who risked their lives every week on the field.

In football, injuries can be a career finisher. Players often hide injuries for the sake of *staying in the game*. A great deal of their understanding of self, personal success, and value is tied to their ability to execute on the playing field, because many find their self-worth on the field. Imagine the sum of your life being tied to every practice, every down, every play, every call. What's at stake is not just a career but an identity.

Football players don't want to lose their roster spot, their position, their value to the team, their fame, their access to financial security. They learn to guard their position with everything they have. So, when the team doctor or coach asks an injured player, "How do you feel? Can you play?" his response might be, "I'm good"; "I'm ready to play"; or "Put me in, Coach!"

Some players have injuries that can't be ignored. Everyone around them—fellow players, team doctors, and the coaching staff—make a commitment to do whatever they can to get that player ready for the next game. Their efforts include cortisone shots, ice baths, bandages, pain medications, technologically advanced pads and helmets, tape, and so on. Permanent healing can become a secondary concern; the priority is winning now. These players sacrifice their bodies and their futures for short-term successes rather than the long-term win—taking time off to permanently heal instead of continually exacerbating old wounds.

You might think, *How egregious. These men are exploited for fame and fortune.* However, many of us have done the same thing. Taking time to heal after a failure or some other wounding is viewed as too costly. We don't want to be sidelined while we await our healing. We'd rather learn to live with pain and develop quick fixes just to get us by. But an intentional commitment to wholeness requires a paradigm shift. We can ascribe value to our identity by how we *stay in the game* versus how we overcome it.

THE GOOD DOCTOR

I love to watch emergency room–related television dramas. They fascinate me. In every show, when a person is bleeding because of an injury, their first thought is to stop the bleeding. Always! The injured person or someone nearby will find whatever they can to stop the bleeding: towels, shirts, jackets, devices to make a tourniquet. But on arrival at any emergency room, the first course of action for the doctor is to immediately remove the makeshift solution in order to inspect the wound.

The doctor views the wound through the lens of a healer: What's wrong? How bad is it? What's been affected by the injury (organs, nerves, bones)? What do I have to do to restore this person to their original condition? God, the Great Physician, views us through the same healer lens. Unlike a doctor, God doesn't have to guess what's wrong. Instead, he zeroes in on what's needed and assesses how he, the Healer, can make us fully whole again.

An untreated physical wound threatens our physical life. An untreated spiritual wound, however, not only threatens our spiritual life but also threatens our leadership identity. God's love for us is so radical that it can bear the worst of our pain (see Isaiah 53:4-5). But we must first choose to remove the makeshift bandages (defense mechanisms and other learned behaviors associated with living in pain) in order to walk through the process of true freedom and thus effectively lead others.

Enduring hardship can feel like a crucible experience—often like death itself. And it *is* death—we are dying to our perception about the infraction(s), and if we have acknowledged God's leadership in our life, we are surrendering to the purpose of God that this hardship will produce.

I know. I feel the weight of those words. Let me explain why.

I met and experienced feelings of love with a man in 2017. We had been introduced through mutual friends. Being introduced to him was unexpected yet refreshing. Our first phone conversation lasted six hours. On our first date I felt like I had known this man forever. By our second date we shared intimate details from our lives and forged a deeper connection. In a restaurant full of people it felt like only three of us were there: God, my date, and me. My heart was beating fast as we talked and were vulnerable to each other.

I asked God, *Who is this man? Is he my husband?* I was overwhelmed with emotion, excitement, and expectation. I didn't want that experience to end. But it did.

A few weeks after we met, he shared that because he had recently divorced, he was not ready for a committed relationship with me. He talked about us, the prayers he'd prayed to God about his future wife, and the amazing woman he viewed me to be, yet he had enough self-awareness to say he was not healed enough to be the type of man he wanted to be for himself and the man he felt I deserved.

I had never before experienced a conversation when a man spent hours explaining to me where he was emotionally. Though I was humbled by his approach and found him to be remarkable, I was confused, devastated, mad at God—a torrent of emotions. He was a breath of fresh air for me—a good communicator, compassionate, personable, tender, loving—but he had been deeply wounded and struggled to reclaim his identity through it all. As we talked, I said some words to him that I'll never forget: "I will not convince you or anyone to be with me. You have to know that for yourself."

Whoa! Only the redeemed Ebony Shanin Small, a woman whose identity was not tied to being in a relationship but anchored in knowing who God already said I was (loved, restored, the apple of his eye), could say that.

He nodded in agreement and asked me to not interpret his pain or process as his rejection of me. Though I *heard* him and really tried not to, inevitably the perceived rejection and pain from past failed relationships soon resurfaced.

A month or so after that conversation, I lashed out at him via text messages. I was heartbroken and depressed yet still leading, serving, preaching, and traveling the world. The saying was true: I didn't look like what I'd been through.

We ended all communication until three months later when he called to tell me he was leaving New York City and moving south. I could feel the tenderness of his heart toward me and was once again devastated, having been holding onto hope that we would be reconciled.

Through it all, the love spoken of in 1 Corinthians 13:4-7 was cultivated within my soul. I made a vow to God in this process: *If my life is in your hands, and all things work together for my good, please reveal to me why you sent this man into my life. Complete the good work you began in me. I vow to not abort this process.* I wanted complete healing.

Years later, God is still doing a work in me that has yet to be completed. Still, I can see some of the results this experience has already produced: through my writing, the many sermons I've preached since then, how I've wrestled with my character, and the counsel I've been privileged to share with broken and hurting people. No makeshift bandages, no temporary solutions—simply God doing what he said he would do!

This is how the crucible of our experiences becomes the platform for our leadership. Another factor in our leadership identity is how equipped we are as leaders after having processed loss. When we do not confront the effect of the loss on our lives, we rob ourselves of the opportunity to grow in our understanding of life's hardships. Doing so is what makes us relatable to others. By embracing every facet of our lives—good and bad—we can lead others authentically.

ASSESSING YOUR LEADERSHIP

Developing our interpersonal skills as leaders is important. Have you ever taken a self-assessment exam as part of the onboarding process for a new job or to gauge your leadership aptitude, spiritual gifting, or readiness as a team player in a work setting? Many resources are available to measure your leadership aptitude, emotional health, define the personality traits that influence your leadership style, and help to uncover possible blind spots in your leadership. Let's go over some of them.

Many clergy and lay leaders have taken an online spiritual gifts assessment based on the list of gifts found in 1 Corinthians 12:28-31, Ephesians 4:7, 11-13, and 1 Peter 4:10-11.

I've completed the following assessments over the past eight years:

- Gallup's CliftonStrengths for individuals, which features four leadership domains and thirty-four themes that assessed my leadership strengths.

- EQ-i 2.0 (Emotional Quotient Inventory) administered by Multi-Health Systems (MHS), which measures emotional health.

- The Highlands Ability Battery administered by the Highlands Company helped me understand how my abilities affect my self-awareness and self-management.

- The Myers-Briggs Type Indicator, a personality inventory featuring sixteen personality types. Taking this test helped me understand how I perceive the world around me and make decisions.

There are many other assessments, but I recommend individuals start with these and process their results with a trained professional. With the Myers-Briggs assessment, I am an ISTJ: Introversion, Sensing, Thinking, Judging. This personality type is described as a quiet and serious person who succeeds by being thorough and dependable. People with this personality type also are described as logical, practical, and resilient—those who take their responsibilities seriously and willingly go beyond the call of duty. They enjoy ordering and structuring their world environment.

All of these descriptors are true of me. It has been deeply affirming to have aspects of my personality lauded and celebrated. I've felt freer to authentically lead as I am rather than having to change myself to fit a mold unnatural to me.

If you're in the New York City area, another leadership development resource is the Advance Leadership Intensive (ALI). This nine-month cohort is offered by Movement.org. "The Advance Leadership Intensive offers faith-based leadership training for Christians engaged in high-level leadership positions within the social sector" and "provides a context for leaders to connect and be equipped, thus enabling organizations throughout the city to flourish."

The ALI leadership team administers the EQ-i 2.0 assessment as part of the program, which has been invaluable to my leadership development. It served to accelerate my thought process when developing my mission-to-measurement plan (a component of the program) as I helped launch a new initiative within the organization. The mission-to-measurement plan helped me to tactically chart how I wanted to grow my ministry (organization or initiative). The plan served me in defining what success looks like while identifying the resources I needed to accomplish these goals.

These previously mentioned assessments and ALI validated my leadership skills and were liberating for me as an introverted leader. Sometimes I have felt deficient in my leadership because I wasn't as outgoing as some colleagues and friends. I also have wished that I could muster the energy to "work a room" and network. But I'd get too drained!

Adam McHugh, the author of *Introverts in the Church*, says, "Leaders must learn to pay attention to their motivations, assumptions, and blind spots. People who are naturally self-reflective have a clear advantage, in this regard, as leaders."

Through these assessments I've embraced my identity and given myself appropriate boundaries. I've learned to value my need for quiet reflection and solitude. These alone times not only refuel me but are the breeding ground for ideas. I accept and celebrate how uniquely God has created me.

LEARNING TO SPEAK UP

I can't remember anyone ever saying, "Ebony, you're a leader!" and then boom, I kicked into high gear. But I can recall opportunities I had to act as a leader.

At the age of thirteen, midway through my freshman year, I transferred to the School of the Future (SOF), an alternative high school in New York City. Alternative schools like SOF didn't require students to take the regents examinations that are required throughout the public school system for grade promotion. I struggled as a test taker, and my exam results did not reflect my knowledge base or comprehension. I am so grateful to my mom for enrolling me at SOF.

At SOF there was a rigorous curriculum coupled with the freedom to generate ideas. The teachers and administrators cultivated this atmosphere to promote student engagement in the learning process and school pride. As a young leader I thrived in this environment.

I started coordinating annual trips to the Six Flags Great Adventures theme park in Jackson, New Jersey, for the entire school. I am amazed by the responsibility my high school principal and teachers allowed me to have as a teenager. I discovered I loved creating experiences in which people could enjoy themselves. For me, that feeling alone was euphoric. My love for event planning began here.

As a member of the second graduating class at my high school, my fellow students and I had the responsibility to create activities to celebrate our senior year. There were no planned events in place. So, with my mom's help, other seniors and I planned the prom. There was no way we could not have a senior prom!

These moments were defining times for me as an emerging leader. I've come to understand that leaders are developed when they have the freedom, space, and a place to dream and act on their ideas with the support of their supervisors.

Yet even as I discovered that I was a leader with influence among my peers, I was hindered by my lack of confidence. As a young adult I continued to struggle with this. In 2009, a few months after I began volunteering for an organization offering free homelessness prevention services to the community, I was asked to design the events journal for their upcoming fundraiser. There was a discrepancy with the journal and the placements of ads which, though I was not at fault, the organization would have been negatively affected by the nonreceipt of some ads. When I tried to explain this to the director, he went off on me. I received such a verbal lashing that I was in shock. I sat there and took it, saying nothing in my defense.

This experience was so wounding I vowed to never work with this organization again. Mostly, I was frustrated with myself and my inability to defend myself. But I discovered that I could not effectively lead others if I didn't exhibit courage in difficult situations.

Many years later I read John Bevere's book *Breaking Intimidation* at the encouragement of one of the elders at my church. The book focused on learning to say no without feeling guilty and to be secure without the approval of others. I asked two friends to read the book along with me, and we prayed together some mornings at 5:00, asking God for help in this area. Slowly, but surely, God answered. I learned to say no through this book and to be honest about my reactions, thoughts, and feelings, professionally and personally.

This book helped me to have difficult conversations and communicate using facts rather than feelings. And God healed me of some deep insecurities and helped me understand that the affirmation people might give me was not the source of my identity. Relationship by relationship, conversation by conversation, I've learned to honor myself and erect boundaries for my self-preservation, which in turn fostered self-respect.

This was part of my journey toward having more authenticity as a leader. Living in the freedom of my identity and embracing the power of my voice has been liberating. Let's talk more about authentic leadership.

DEVELOPING AUTHENTIC LEADERSHIP

Authentic leadership is the ability to be emotionally healthy and committed to courageously pursuing truth in our lives so we are not hindered as we lead others to uncover the truth of their own identity.

Sam Chand is an Atlanta-based leadership architect and consultant as well as the author of *Bigger, Faster Leadership*. I heard him speak at the United Pentecostal Council of the Assemblies of God National Conference in 2017. During that conference Chand shared that the first responsibility of a leader is to define reality in order to accurately assess needs and demonstrate authentic leadership in ways that inspire others to meet goals, effectuate change, and leave an indelible impression in the places they are called to lead.

The characteristics of this level of leadership—emotional healthiness, confidence, and influence—don't come overnight but are cultivated through an intentional commitment to pursue truth and lead in that truth.

My goal is to live as an authentic leader. In a culture of great falsity, where photoshopped images daily distort our perceptions of reality, where does truth actually live? Can we trust what we see? What we hear? Even if the information comes from seemingly trusted sources, where does truth *really* begin and end?

There's often an agenda behind the information presented to us. I daily feel the need to dig deeper to understand the issues and discern the next steps. This can't be done apart from the Holy

Spirit. I'm grateful for the resources God has provided to help me learn how to be more discerning.

One of those resources is the Q Conference in Nashville. I've had the pleasure to be a guest speaker at pre-events for this conference for the past four years. The Q stands for "questions," and this conference helps educate church and cultural leaders to showcase publicly the ways of the gospel while thoughtfully navigating today's culture.

We all have inherent biases rooted in family tradition and life experiences. Conferences like the Q Conference enable discussion of hot-button issues and our perceptions about them. This conference reminds me of how important it is for a leader to root out any hidden biases to avoid wounding the people he or she serves.

At Q 2018, Michael Wear gave a talk on reclaiming hope. Michael is the founder of Public Square Strategies, a consulting firm that helps businesses, nonprofits, foundations, and Christian organizations to weather the changing thoughts concerning faith, politics, and culture. Wear directed the faith outreach for President Obama's 2012 reelection campaign and was one of the youngest White House staffers in modern American history as he helped manage the White House's engagement on religious and values issues, including adoption and anti-human trafficking efforts. In his talk at Q, Michael discussed identity politics and identity religious beliefs. *Identity politics* speaks to when we derive our identity from political affiliations and change what we believe to fit the varied cultural moments. *Identity religious belief* refers to when people go to politics to get their spiritual needs met. This can cause great spiritual harm because the person's identity is not rooted in the godly character derived from God's Word but instead is in the fleeting viewpoints of humans.

As Michael explained, a Christian's obligation is not to a political tribe but to the God who causes leaders to work toward the benefit of all people. This God cares deeply for people. Wear admonished Christians to be concerned about a church that fears the power of culture more than the power of God. For Christians the mandate should be to turn to the political arena to advance justice rather than turning to this arena for a spiritual identity.

Authentic leadership doesn't require that we become chameleons that conform to every manner of doctrine but rather to stand firm in our intrinsic beliefs even if they're deeply rooted in faith that might not be culturally popular.

Our lives are filled with an abundance of memories and experiences, some deeply painful, others profoundly joyful, as well as people who've left lasting impressions on us, including mentors who've helped shape our thinking. We must learn from the painful experiences in our lives but not lead from them. All of these experiences are essential for our growth, and through them we come to experience new depths in our character and leadership that we might not have otherwise known.

REFLECTION QUESTIONS

1. How has your leadership identity been shaped by your experiences?

2. What personality/leadership assessments have you taken? How have they helped you in your pursuit of ministry or other leadership opportunities?

3. What challenges have you faced in your desire to lead authentically?

4. How would you describe your worldview?

5. How does your worldview inform how you lead?

6. Who in your life helps you to truthfully assess the possibility of hidden biases?

CHAPTER FOUR

SURRENDERING ALL

Take my heart and form it
Take my mind, transform it.

Scott Underwood, "Take My Life"

WHAT DO YOU WANT TO BE WHEN YOU GROW UP?" This is the age-old question every child is asked. I wanted to be an obstetrician/gynecologist for as long as I can remember. I don't know when my fascination with medicine began. When I was fifteen, I volunteered at the Lenox Hill Hospital's Labor and Delivery Unit (New York City). This was one of the most exciting times of my life. I was passionate about pursuing a career in medicine.

During my senior year of high school, I enrolled in the Bridge to Medicine (BTM) program offered through the City University of New York (CUNY). On weekdays I spent my mornings at high school and then traveled to Harlem in the afternoon for classes on CUNY's campus. BTM was designed to help minority students who planned to enter the rigorous premedicine programs during their freshman year of college.

Upon completing BTM and enrolling in the State University of New York at Binghamton, I set out to complete my general education credit requirements as I started the pre-med course track.

Against the advice of my mom and my college adviser, I registered to take intro-level courses in biology, chemistry, psychology, and general literature. Uh, yeah! While I aced my general literature course, I received a D in psychology and failed biology and chemistry. At the end of my first semester, I was on academic probation with a 1.7 GPA.

These grades were a major shock and rattled my faith in my future. Though I knew I could handle college-level course work, I would need additional help for the required science classes. So, I decided that as much as I wanted to be a doctor, I was not committed to the hard work required to succeed in that field.

At the beginning of my sophomore year I changed my major to pre-law but didn't stick with that major long. In fact, I wasn't clear about my future. I switched to African American studies with a minor in sociology. I graduated and began my professional career working for Big Brothers Big Sisters of New York City (BBBS) by way of referral from a Binghamton alum. Big Brothers Big Sisters is considered to be the founding agency for the youth mentoring movement in the United States.

During college I didn't pursue opportunities for leadership within student associations but did join the Pi Eta chapter of Delta Sigma Theta Sorority in the spring of my sophomore year. I was in search of a sisterhood to fuel and hone my desire to serve the local community. Through our chapter we led many amazing programs, but for some reason I didn't find my stride as a leader by fully investing in our chapter. I wish I could have served better. BBBS also promoted leadership, creativity, and the freedom to execute ideas. I began to dream again and thrive in opportunities to plan meaningful special events for our "bigs" (mentors) and "littles" (mentees). I also began to explore my skills as a volunteer trainer with the BBBS Center for Training.

I was so satisfied with my work that I never missed a day in three years (other than vacation time). My work was rewarding, and I was valued by my directors and colleagues. Yet faith in God didn't play a part in my day-to-day decision making. While I identified as a Christian, I wasn't focused on a relationship with God at that time.

When I left BBBS, I worked for other nonprofits: Good Shepherd Services, AIDS Center of Queens County, and Memorial Sloan-Kettering Cancer Center. In the midst of these opportunities I followed my dream of becoming an entrepreneur by starting Longevity Wedding Consultants (LWC) in 2005. Though I worked full-time, for ten years I also planned weddings and special events. I closed the business in December 2015, sensing that I needed to make more room in my life for what God wanted to add.

MY LIFE OR HIS LIFE?

The ability to sense the timing of God's movement in my life first began with my willingness to listen to his voice and yield to his direction.

When I was asked what I wanted to be when I grew up, I responded the way I saw myself: as the owner of my life. *My* life's plan started off as a desire to become a doctor. But then the plan changed to becoming a lawyer, then to just getting a job, then becoming a wedding planner. I wanted to become a famous wedding planner—the next Preston Bailey, David Tutera, or Diann Valentine.

You know that other age-old question asked during job interviews: "Where do you see yourself in the next five years?" I could answer you! I wanted to be a successful, established leader who was financially secure. But that ambition changed when I discovered a radical relationship with God.

In 2005, *my* life became *his* life. It belonged to him already. I surrendered my life wholeheartedly to God. I *gave up* the right to make decisions about my career, where I would live, and so on, without consulting God first. I *gave up* my right to choose the person I would date and marry. I *gave in*—surrendered to the fact that my understanding was not supreme, and I yielded forever to God's infinite wisdom.

In order to find *my life*, I had to lay it down, as Jesus described in Matthew 16:24-25. And the promises of God began to unlock a future for me that I could never have opened.

ALL IN!

In an article titled "What Difference Does Scripture Engagement Make?" at the American Bible Society website, writer Carolyn Wildermuth discovered that consistent interaction with God's Word reshapes our choices and transforms our relationships with God and others, making us into people who naturally put into practice the two great commandments Jesus spoke of in Matthew 22:37-40.

When you're in a relationship with someone, you consider that person's needs and wants. You want to do what pleases them. What brings that person joy brings you joy. Paul in his first letter to the church of Corinth described this devotion to the Lord:

> I would like you to be free from concern. An unmarried man is concerned about the Lord's affairs—how he can please the Lord. But a married man is concerned about the affairs of this world—how he can please his wife—and his interests are divided. An unmarried woman or virgin is concerned about the Lord's affairs: Her aim is to be devoted to the Lord in both body and spirit. But a married woman is concerned about the affairs of this world—how she can please her

husband. I am saying this for your own good, not to restrict you, but that you may live in a right way in undivided devotion to the Lord. (1 Corinthians 7:32-35)

I understand Paul's depiction of this struggle. When we are not focused on the spiritual matters of our life, but later discover that God is our anchor, we want to maintain this new mindset. We don't want our relationship with God to be hindered by anyone or anything. That's how it has been for me for the past fourteen years. I've determined that there are places I simply don't want to go to anymore—places I used to enjoy. There are conversations I don't want to have about petty things and invitations I've had to decline.

In the first year of my rededication to God (2005–2006), I know I hurt a lot of people I love. I withdrew from many friendships and became more focused on building my faith. In my withdrawal from others I wasn't able to articulate that I was literally in the battle for my life—my spiritual life. Would they have understood anyway? First Corinthians 2:14 tells us, "The person without the Spirit does not accept the things that come from the Spirit of God but considers them foolishness, and cannot understand them because they are discerned only through the Spirit."

As I've lamented the lack of closeness or even the complete loss of these relationships, I've learned to avoid condemning myself for not having had a better balance of maintaining my relationships while growing spiritually. I could have tried to explain more what was happening in my life during that time. Still, I can't help feeling pain when I see on social media that I wasn't invited to a wedding, baby shower, birthday, or other life events because the friendship is not as strong as it once was.

God has allowed some relationships to be restored, but many are not. He is still healing me in this area. I trust that one day there won't be the twinge of hurt or rejection when a joyous event comes across my social media feed that I was not invited to. Instead, I can express thankfulness to the Lord for blessing someone who still means so much to me.

When we surrender our lives to God, it will cost us something. As we become intoxicated by the Lord's presence, we will sacrifice to pursue his will because all we want is more of him.

I've learned to uphold the daily process of surrender in my life by incorporating the spiritual disciplines of prayer, Scripture reading, weekly fellowship with the body of Christ through my local church, and engaging in mentoring relationships. I'm committed to lifelong learning.

Two books have helped me in my spiritual formation: Richard Foster's *Celebration of Discipline* and *The Practice of the Presence of God* by Brother Lawrence. Incorporating spiritual disciplines has informed my life's choices and leadership. As I've embraced my life in Christ as a gift and accepted that my choices are a part of God's will, every sphere of influence God has placed me in has become a place of significant purpose and value. With that understanding I've approached every leadership responsibility God has given me with the same questions I asked when I surrendered my life to God: *God, what is your will? What is your purpose for me here?* These questions have become a necessary anchor as I yield my leadership to God's intended purpose. I'm led by a strong sense that I have been sent by God in humility to serve the needs of his people.

A past leader, one I greatly admire, was sent with that purpose in mind.

LEADING ON PURPOSE

In 1797, Isabella Baumfree was born into a life of slavery in Ulster, New York. She was sold at the age of nine for $100. This wouldn't be the first or the last time she would be bought and sold. During her enslavement she was subject to harsh physical treatment. Though she fell in love with a man named Robert from another farm, they were forbidden to marry because they had separate owners. Isabella was forced to marry a man named Thomas, with whom she bore five children.

Incredible hardship continued to plague Isabella's life. As New York began the slow process to emancipate its slaves, Isabella began to petition for her freedom from her current slave-master, John Dumont. He initially promised to let her go, but then reneged.

Isabella escaped with her infant daughter, regretfully leaving her other four children behind. Upon arriving in New Paltz, New York, she found shelter with the Van Wagenen family, who offered to redeem her life by paying $20 to her slave owner when he came to reclaim her.

Out of spite, Dumont illegally sold Isabella's son back into slavery due to reversals in the state legislature that allowed for this, but with the help of the Van Wagenens, Isabella filed a lawsuit to reclaim her son. She was the first African American woman to sue a Caucasian man in the United States, a case she won.

The blessing of this family to Isabella had far greater implications: she became a strong believer in Jesus during her time with them. As she grew in her knowledge of God's will for her life, she was convicted by God to speak the truth. She *gave up* the identity of her former life and *gave in* to what she believed was God's direction for her life: that she preach the gospel and speak out against slavery. So, in 1843, with this new direction in her life, she changed her name to Sojourner Truth.

Sojourner Truth has been an example to me of strength, courage, determination, and purposeful leadership in the face of persecution and profound hardship. At her point of surrender to

God, she was able to take up a far greater calling than she probably ever envisioned for herself. I can imagine with every yes to God's plan, with every comfort he required her to surrender to him, with time spent away from family and friends, she actualized the abundance and depth of God's will for her life.

It is remarkable what the power of surrendering all can produce in us. Sojourner became an abolitionist and a champion of the rights of women and all humans. One of the most famous speeches she delivered at a women's rights convention in 1851 was titled "Ain't I a Woman?" In it she observes,

> Then that little man in black there, he says women can't have as much rights as men, 'cause Christ wasn't a woman! Where did your Christ come from? Where did your Christ come from? From God and a woman! Man had nothing to do with him.

Until the time of her death in 1883, Sojourner courageously appealed for the abolition of slavery, sought to find jobs for freed African Americans following the Civil War, and promoted women's rights. She was recognized for her activism and was invited to meet President Abraham Lincoln. Her faith in God gave her a voice and platform that has had generational implications.

Ponder that reality. Our yes to God has generational implications. There's something about surrendering to God that adds volume to our life, power to our voice, and power to accomplish his purposes—God's kingdom come, God's will be done. This reminds me of Acts 1:8: "You will receive power when the Holy Spirit comes on you; and you will be my witnesses in Jerusalem, and in all Judea and Samaria, and to the ends of the earth."

As my identity in God has become increasingly secure in his purpose for my life, he's filled me from the inside out to live as a leader who intentionally invests in the people God has called me to lead and serve.

LEADERS: BORN OR MADE?

Though famed football player and NFL executive Vince Lombardi said, "Leaders are made, they are not born," the first person I heard using a version of this statement was Marie-Yolaine Toms in a video endorsement for Movement Day, which we filmed in 2012. Marie-Yolaine is CEO and Fire Starter of Community-2Community (C2C), a nonprofit dedicated to creating self-sufficient communities in Haiti.

I had met Marie years earlier through two deacons of my church, Calvin and Marcia Hawkins. Marie held a monthly meeting at her home in Brooklyn and was a member of the Christian Cultural Center in Brooklyn. I learned so much from Marie, who is an amazing woman of God. She became the friend I needed early in my faith journey when I was trying to find my identity. And she was the first Christian I had met who held Christian fellowships in her home.

During those meetings we would worship, share, and pray for each other. Marie modeled what I now love to do in my home: invite fellow believers to worship God, study the Word, share transparently, pray fervently, and experience the freedom of God's blessing and deliverance within community. Marie's purposeful leadership and surrender to God has forever changed my life.

In her video interview for Movement Day, Marie shares that after the 2010 earthquake in Haiti she was frustrated by the piecemeal approach that aid was being administered. She wondered when someone would do something to help this. That someone turned out to be her. Marie resigned from her job and was sponsored by a friend to attend Movement Day in 2011. There she participated in the breakout session on rebuilding Haiti. During this time Marie launched C2C. She learned the power of collaboration through talks at Movement Day, which helped deepen her organizational leadership understanding. She has since shared with others the tools she learned at Movement Day and has witnessed the life-changing impact of these principles. Marie's yes to God is having generational implications as she works to resource a nation and empower people.

According to an article written by Elizabeth Powitzky on a study conducted by *Forbes* magazine, if you believe that leaders are not born but made, you're in good company. Thirty percent of those polled believe leaders are born, while 70 percent believe leadership ability is formed through life experiences. In other words, they are made.

While analyzing this research in a 2014 study, Kari Keating, David Rosch, and Lisa Burgoon, professors at the University of Illinois, discovered an efficient way to develop leaders. First, they studied students in a fifteen-week introductory course on leadership development. The professors discerned that the progress the students experienced was the product of being ready, willing, and able. "Students first become ready to learn about being a leader; then they become willing to learn the skills necessary to practice leadership; and finally, they're able to lead because they have the skills and the motivation to do it," Rosch explained.

Their findings reflect my leadership journey and are descriptive of many other leaders like Sojourner Truth and Marie-Yolaine Toms, whose conviction in God's great power motivated them to intentionally surrender their desires to God's plan.

Surrendering all to God revolutionizes our life in ways we cannot imagine. First Corinthians 2:9 states,

> But as it is written:
> "Eye has not seen, nor ear heard,
> Nor have entered into the heart of man

The things which God has prepared for those who love
Him." (NKJV)

We can't fathom that which God has prepared for us.

REFLECTION QUESTIONS

1. What does it mean to you to surrender to God? Why?

2. Which of the types of surrender discussed in this chapter have you noticed in your life? What does this inspire in you?

3. How have you demonstrated to God by your actions that you are "all in"?

4. Where and how are you intentionally investing your leadership?

PART TWO

LEADERSHIP SPECIFICS

CHAPTER FIVE

GOD'S CALLING VERSUS MY ABILITY

The LORD came and stood there,
calling as at the other times, "Samuel! Samuel!"
Then Samuel said, "Speak, for your servant is listening."

1 SAMUEL 3:10

WHEN I THINK OF GOD'S CALL ON A LIFE, I can't help thinking of the prophets in the Bible. Prophets like Samuel. But his mother's act of diligent prayer set the stage for the direction of his life. Samuel was dedicated to the Lord as a baby by his mother, Hannah. This act of dedication was in keeping with Hannah's vow to God before she conceived. Having been barren for many years, she *needed* God to answer her prayer for a son (1 Samuel 1).

Have you ever felt this level of desperation?

Hannah vowed that if she had a son, she would give that child back to God to serve him all the days of the child's life. What a deeply sacrificial prayer. God answered her prayer by enabling her to conceive. Thus, Samuel was born. I can only imagine Hannah's joy at being honored by God in this way. Hannah and her husband, Elkanah, gave Samuel to the priest Eli at the tabernacle, where Samuel remained in the service of the Lord.

At the tabernacle, even as a young child, Samuel was devoted to serving God with Eli the priest. If you went to Sunday school as a child, you probably know the story. Samuel heard a voice calling his name. It had to be Eli, right? But Eli assured Samuel that God was calling. Later, God spoke these words to Samuel:

> I am about to do a shocking thing in Israel. I am going to carry out all my threats against Eli and his family, from beginning to end. I have warned him that judgment is coming upon his family forever, because his sons are blaspheming God and he hasn't disciplined them. So I have vowed that the sins of Eli and his sons will never be forgiven by sacrifices or offerings. (1 Samuel 3:11-14 NLT)

When Eli asked Samuel what God told him, charging him to avoid holding back anything, Samuel told him everything. Imagine hearing what Eli heard, but about *your* family. How would you react? Yet Eli accepted this devastating news.

Samuel was a renowned prophet throughout Israel. He also was the last in the line of Israel's judges—the leaders chosen by God after the death of Joshua to lead the people against their enemies (see the book of Judges).

Throughout history God has spoken to people audibly, through the Holy Spirit, through his Word, through prophets, and through others who serve him. There is no limit to the ways God speaks to his people.

Have you ever had to give someone bad news and attempted to soften the blow? Samuel's example of telling Eli exactly what God said instead of sugarcoating it is an important lesson for us to learn. When God speaks to us about ourselves or has a revelation for someone else of things to come, we must not hold back in an attempt to shield ourselves from a bad reaction to the message. The more we hear God's voice and respond in obedience, the stronger we'll become as we stand before others as his messenger.

WHOSE VOICE DO YOU HEED?

Some people doubt the existence of God, let alone the fact that God speaks to people. Yet in John 10:27, Jesus provides this assurance: "My sheep listen to my voice; I know them, and they follow me." God yearns to have a relationship with all people and desires to impart wisdom and direction to those who seek him. As promised in Jeremiah 33:3: "Call to me and I will answer you and tell you great and unsearchable things you do not know." When followers of Jesus call to him, he promises to answer.

God also responds to faith: "Without faith it is impossible to please God, because anyone who comes to him must believe that he exists and that he rewards those who earnestly seek him" (Hebrews 11:6).

When we who believe ask for God's direction, the testing of our faith comes with our ability to wait for his response. Over the years I've learned that waiting for God doesn't mean he didn't hear my prayer the first time or that he's too busy to respond. His timing, which differs from mine, is perfect.

Many voices vie for supremacy in our lives—family, well-meaning friends, our own reasonings and deductions, our busy lives, and the urge for immediate information. Those without faith might add other sources they believe will provide direction; for example, psychics, horoscopes, or religious rituals suggested by others.

Whose advice has precedence in your life? Our actions reveal the adviser we most respect. If God, then those actions will bear godly fruit.

Trusting God includes yielding to his desires for our lives, which are discerned through the Holy Spirit (John 14:26). We can know those desires through maintaining a relationship with God through prayer and studying the Bible.

I have learned how to hear the voice of God. The first time God spoke to me was through a passage in the Bible. I have had experiences when I talked to God and heard his voice within my spirit. I have yet to experience God speaking to me in the detailed way he spoke to Samuel. But each time he's spoken has been an incredible gift.

God might speak to you about a prayer request, about Jesus, or about a particular call on your life. If he has chosen to speak to you about his call to greater surrender and service, he might do so over a period of time through various life-defining experiences. Let's talk more about God's call.

GOD'S CALLING

To be called by God is to be chosen to perform a specific leadership assignment. The Bible is full of stories of people called to be prophets (for example, Samuel, Isaiah, and Jeremiah), judges (Deborah and Gideon) or deliverers (Moses). Often this calling is well beyond any duty the chosen person could have imagined undertaking. This person has to rely on the Holy Spirit's counsel and strength to accomplish the assignment.

The call of God has to be accepted. So, what are the requirements for accepting a call? First, submit to God's plans. Considering your own comfort or self-preservation takes a backseat to what God requires. Second, be obedient. Do what God says for you to do.

It takes great courage to follow God and embark on a journey blind. But peace can be found in the fact that God's plans for his people are good (see Jeremiah 29:11).

Wealth, status, and power are the currency of this earthly kingdom. Obedience, faith, and submission are the currency of

God's kingdom. You will never actualize the call of God without these.

Scripture doesn't mention that God told Samuel directly that he would be a prophet and a judge. God invited Samuel first into a relationship. Through Samuel's obedience God established Samuel's position. With each act of obedience—prophesying as instructed, counseling people, leading Israel to victory over their enemies, judging righteously—Samuel's platform increased. He also was given the task of choosing Israel's first king. The people demanded a king because of Samuel's old age and the inability of his sons to lead with integrity (1 Samuel 8). Kings would now take the place of the judges. God identified Saul as the future king and sent Samuel to appoint him.

Not everyone willingly accepts God's call. God wanted the prophet Jonah to go to Nineveh to preach a message of repentance. Jonah, however, boarded a ship to Tarshish, which was in the opposite direction of Nineveh, hoping to escape from the Lord (see Jonah 1).

Sometimes we attempt to escape God's direction. Though I haven't tried to run from God in the way Jonah did, one of my greatest struggles has been dealing with feelings of inadequacy. I continually remind myself that while perfection is never my goal, excellence in any assignment is always attainable and can be reached by how diligently I prepare.

Jonah remained in the belly of the fish for three days and three nights. There, Jonah prayed to the Lord, acknowledging God's mercy despite his disobedience. He surrendered to God's will, saying,

I will offer sacrifices to you with songs of praise,
    and I will fulfill all my vows.
    For my salvation comes from the LORD alone.
        (Jonah 2:9 NLT)

Once the fish spit Jonah out, he was ready to obey. God could have killed Jonah and sent another messenger to Nineveh. But this story reminds us that God extends his mercy even when we don't quickly obey.

ARE YOU ABLE OR CALLED?

In 2005, once I was certain that God had called me to serve at Bethel Gospel Assembly, I met with our senior pastor, Pastor Brown (now Bishop Brown), and shared that I wanted to serve in ministry and asked him to place me where he best saw fit. I offered for his consideration the natural abilities I possessed: event planning, strategic planning, effective administrator, research driven, self-motivation, flexible, quick learner, and excellent work ethic. Being the wise and discerning pastor that he is, Pastor Brown called the church's business administrator, Michelle P. Robinson, into his office. From that point on I began a five-year period of service with Michelle, learning the business of conducting ministry.

I also served on the intercessory prayer team, the audio/visual ministry, the trustee committee, member services, Alabaster Women of Faith, and ministry relations. In my early journey of service, I was finding my footing in ministry as I learned my spiritual gifts and how to serve and lead others, and discovered my areas of passion. Initially, I lacked a distinct sense of call to one particular area of ministry. But even as I waited for God to reveal his areas of calling for me, I was determined to be active. So, when I made photocopies, videotaped announcements, prayed during a service, taught a new believer's class, I did so out of gratefulness to God for saving my soul and my life.

As we wait patiently for God's direction in our lives, we need to make ourselves available for his kingdom work. Don't sit idly on the sidelines watching others tirelessly serve until all the pieces of the puzzle come together for you. Remember the ten lepers Jesus healed! They didn't wait for the healing to take place; they responded to Jesus' word by going and were healed by faith (Luke 17:14). Explore some options for ministry. As we demonstrate an active trust that God will direct us when he's ready, we can prayerfully fulfill our vows to be lifelong servants by doing whatever tasks we find to do.

ON-THE-JOB TRAINING

In 2006, during a MasterLife Bible study class at Bethel, a nine-month discipleship course aimed at helping participants to deepen their relationship with God, I took my first spiritual gifts test and discovered that I have the following gifts (some were uncovered over time): leadership, administration, exhortation, healing, discerning spirits, word of knowledge, word of wisdom, faith, speaking in tongues, ministry/service, hospitality, intercession, pastoral guidance, and teaching.

To become a doctor, a person needs to be trained in medical school. Police officers are trained at the police academy, and lawyers gain knowledge through law school and internships at law firms. For jobs that don't require professional training or schooling, individuals receive on-the-job training. Every assignment requires training of some kind. Our training and abilities empower us to accomplish the tasks set before us. Believers' training and spiritual gifts are the fuel God uses to empower us to establish the kingdom of God on earth as it is in heaven.

Leading the Alabaster Women of Faith's (AWOF) empowerment group, beginning in 2008, was the first time I had experienced God's calling in an area of leadership. The assignment to lead these women was not something I had imagined would happen. I felt grossly unqualified and had to rely on God's wisdom and strength to sustain me. As I walked in obedience and invested in the lives of these women, my ministry of preaching and teaching unfolded.

This period of my life was exhilarating. The joy of seeing lives transformed enlivened me. I was passionate about serving in this ministry. No matter my circumstances, I was at Bethel's Praise Chapel on Thursday evenings to empower others even as I awaited God's direction in my own life.

As a result of my faithfulness during this season of leading AWOF and being underemployed, God opened the door for me to work at Movement.org full time. With Movement.org I flourished in other areas of leadership as an administrator, mentor, executive, coach, communicator, and connector of people and networks. God has used my years of on-the-job training as an events director and administrator to plan large catalytic events that serve to accelerate gospel movements in cities. It has been one of the greatest honors of my life to serve God in this way. But my passion is to be a disciple maker and a communicator. I seek opportunities to invest in younger leaders through one-on-one mentorship and discipleship. I never consider these assignments burdensome; they are deeply fulfilling.

I discovered my passion for discipling the next generation of younger leaders in 2013 after I was ordained as an elder at Bethel. That time Bishop Brown asked me to give leadership to a new auxiliary ministry, Third Service.

Third Service was intended to be an alternative youth and young adult worship service on the third Saturday of every month. Following the example of other ministry leaders, I established a team of younger leaders to serve alongside me in launching this ministry. In each member of the team I saw the gift of leadership as evidenced by their great influence among their peers. As I mentored them, they challenged me to refine the goals for Third Service to ensure that the service was youth led rather than another rigid religious activity.

I learned to listen intently to the team's ideas and even created ministry planning meetings to uncover their ideas for how we could advance the mission of the ministry. Meeting with them became the highlight of my month. Serving with them was one of my greatest joys. Every time I look at them, I thank God for helping me to be passionate about serving them.

After watching them blossom, I took on the role of ministry overseer, leaving the day-to-day leadership to the team. Meanwhile, God affirmed my calling to younger leaders by connecting me with two other youth ministries at Kings Highway United Methodist Church in Brooklyn, New York, and Grace United Methodist Church in Queens, New York, under the leadership of Rev. Dr. Chermain Lashley. For the past five years I've preached regularly at their youth and women's retreats. Being around youth who are hungry for God has pushed me to become a better servant and leader. They will tell you how much I've influenced them, but their impact on my life has been invaluable.

I remember being frustrated every time someone asked me what I was passionate about, and I had to admit that I had no idea. How about you? Are you feeling this way? Uncovering your passion(s) will take prayer and time. Some people know their passion(s) all their lives; the rest of us have to wait for God's revelation. While you wait, remember that you don't lack purpose. You can get help to uncover your areas of passion. You might choose to enroll in a program like Henry Cloud and John Townsend's Growth Skills workshop. This workshop helps people define the skills needed to reach their goals.

Most of us know people who work a nine-to-five job just to make a living, but who also have side jobs, hobbies, or other activities that are deeply fulfilling. Passion and calling elicit this level of joy and fulfillment. The apostle Paul was a tentmaker by vocation (Acts 18:3) but was chosen by God to spread the gospel as a missionary to the Gentiles. Like Jesus, Paul's food was to do the will of the One who sent him. He demonstrated conviction in carrying out this call. Regarding this, Paul explained,

> I have done the Lord's work humbly and with many tears. I have endured the trials that came to me from the plots of the Jews. I never shrank back from telling you what you needed to hear, either publicly or in your homes. I have had one message for Jews and Greeks alike—the necessity of repenting from sin and turning to God, and of having faith in our Lord Jesus. (Acts 20:19-21 NLT)

Paul was empowered by God to preach and lead many to repentance. His life and the letters he wrote are still revered thousands of years after his death. Many lives have been changed as a result of his courage to obey God's call on his life.

Do we have that courage? I hope Paul's example encourages us to say yes and submit to God, no matter what he calls us to do or no matter how difficult that call might seem. There is an eternal glory to be revealed by our obedience.

I had to make this decision for myself.

NOT ME, LORD!

Years ago, when Pastor Brown's wife, Pastor Lorna, prophesied over me during a morning worship service on New Year's Eve, she said that part of the vision our senior pastor had was for missionaries to be sent from the church globally by the year 2020. She believed I would be one of those missionaries.

I immediately started to cry. These were not tears of joy and thanksgiving but a lament as I thought of how my life would change. I imagined God would send me to a foreign country to live in a remote village. How would I get my hair done? I know, totally not spiritual, right? But it's the truth. Yet that prophetic word came to pass. Through my work at Movement.org, I've traveled to countries in Africa, the United Kingdom, Indonesia, India, and countless US cities advancing God's kingdom. I have spent so much time flying that flight attendants are becoming familiar.

To be a missionary doesn't just involve getting on a plane, however. We can be missionaries to our community. God's call is not just for pastors, preachers, and teachers. God raises up leaders in every sphere of influence. The unilateral qualifiers are salvation and surrender. God will never force you to do an assignment.

You might think, *Well wasn't Jonah forced?* Jonah wasn't forced—Jonah was afraid. The prayer he uttered to God from the belly of the fish didn't convey a begrudging yes but instead expressed worship to God for salvation as well as a submission to God's call (see Jonah 2).

When we have the reputation of capable leaders, we will get asked to help with many projects. As we pray about these opportunities, we can pray also about any people-pleasing tendencies we have in this area. Otherwise, we'll say yes to every request and be sapped of the capacity to lead effectively in the places we've been uniquely called to.

For years I struggled with people pleasing and sometimes found myself committing to tasks I lacked passion for. For example, in 2012 I was asked to help plan a silent auction fundraiser for a local NYC organization. I said yes to the project without seeking God's direction and also with an awareness that the leader of the organization was difficult to work with. My enthusiasm for the project quickly waned. I dreaded the responsibility of having to plan the event. As expected, working with a challenging personality type was difficult. The event was moderately successful, but how much better might it have been with a passionate team behind it?

When we're passionate, we go above and beyond to complete our assignments. We tirelessly and sacrificially give of ourselves. By accepting assignments we're only moderately interested in, we might achieve only moderate results that a called leader might have avoided.

THE POWER OF A GODLY INFLUENCE

Samuel's mother directed the course of his life because of her faith in God. Before he was born, his mother had decided that Samuel would be a lifelong servant of God. That's powerful.

Likewise, God's plan for our lives was already established before we were born (Psalm 139:16). We come into agreement with that plan by virtue of our salvation and surrender. If I had not surrendered to God in 2005, I would not be the author of this book, nor would I have experienced many of the life events described in this book. That's mind blowing to me.

Can you imagine the millions of people who have missed the plans of God for their lives because they've never been taught about God, or, far worse, they've heard the gospel message but didn't receive him? Think about how many graves are filled with unreached potential.

As God had planned for a fish to consume Jonah during that great storm, God will identify the people, places, and even animals he can use to serve as refiners or incubators for his calling in our lives. Throughout the Scriptures there were apostles, prophets, pastors, teachers, and evangelists sent by God to commission others for works of service.

When the people of Israel asked God for a king, God identified Saul and sent Samuel to anoint Saul for this divine service (1 Samuel 10). Samuel was a refiner in Saul's life, one that Saul ignored (1 Samuel 13; 15). After all, Samuel gave Saul orders that Saul ignored, thus causing God to anoint someone else.

The Scriptures and critical life events can lead us to a place of prayer, where we surrender to God's plan, a plan far greater than our own. There will also be those who affirm God's call in our lives by opening doors for us to have a wider influence. God has used countless people to position, encourage, or equip me in his calling. As an example of this, my first preaching invitation came from a participant in AWOF's empowerment group.

The right mix of pain, despair, and uncertainty can awaken us to our need for salvation, and influence us to acknowledge that there is a God with greater power than we could ever muster. The perfect storm came into my life in 2005 in the form of a dysfunctional relationship, the death of a family member, depression, and loneliness, which led me to pick up my Bible and search for answers. God worked within these life events to change the trajectory of my life.

God can use people to change the trajectory of a life. One such person is Mac Pier, the founder of Movement.org. Over thirty years ago Mac and his wife, Marya, moved to New York City from South Dakota. During an Urbana Missions Conference, they felt commissioned by God to serve as missionaries in NYC. Upon arriving in New York more than twenty-five years ago, Mac founded Concerts of Prayer Greater New York. Today, thousands of pastors have convened in monthly prayer meetings and summits. From these gatherings of pray-ers these leaders have deepened relationships with each other, which accelerated God's mission and plan for NYC.

In 2008, Mac and a few others started the New York City Leadership Center (NYCLC) in response to a survey of pastors who had indicated their desire for more practical urban ministry training, something their seminaries had not prepared them for. At NYCLC, now Movement.org, the Advance Leadership Intensive (ALI) was launched to serve these pastors. Movement Day was launched in 2010 to catalyze Christian leaders to spiritually and socially influence their city.

I have not met many leaders quite like Mac, who daily shows those around him the transformative call of God to reach the global church. He is a visionary leader with a vast network of ministry partners and friends. He often brings gifted leaders together to consider what God might call them to do in unity to advance God's kingdom. He also empowers younger leaders to be effective and courageous. I am one such leader.

I've watched him single-handedly encourage leaders who barely knew each other to commit to meaningful ministry together.

In September 2010, the Movement Day gathering in NYC consisted of eight hundred leaders. In 2019, this gathering has expanded across five continents with over thirty thousand leaders trained. And the collective impact of the now over four hundred alumni of ALI has transformed hundreds of thousands of local leaders.

Mac and his family are also deeply sacrificial. He's a tireless fundraiser. For many years he spent three weeks of every month traveling the world to meet network leaders and investors, and to serve as an ambassador of Movement Day as well as an encourager of those pursuing God's call. He always takes time to respond to anyone who wants to hear his testimony or wants advice to refine a personal mission.

In July 2011, Mac interviewed me for the events manager role at Movement.org. He also affirmed my promotion to director of Movement Day and Events in 2014 and then to director of Movement Day Expressions in 2017. He nominated me to serve alongside him as a Co-Catalyst for Cities with the Lausanne Movement and as a board member for the Table Coalition (formerly Mission America Coalition). He has been a divinely appointed accelerator in my life as God uncovered areas of passion and calling in my leadership. Many other leaders also have credited Mac's Holy Spirit-led influence in the process of accelerating their leadership investment in God's kingdom.

God's call puts us in places where we can influence the destiny of people and nations. We become grafted into a kingdom agenda that existed before the foundations of the earth were laid. God's call fulfills us from the inside out and allows our lives to bring forth a harvest that will bless generations of our family to come.

As we continue in our service to God, we do so with great thanksgiving and joy. We serve with boldness and faithfulness. Heaven will tell the story of all we've done.

REFLECTION QUESTIONS

1. What are your abilities and spiritual gifts?

2. Where do you sense God's call to serve?

3. How has your calling been affirmed by others?

4. Are you being mentored in this area? What are the other areas where you might need to grow?

5. Have you discovered your area of passion? If so, what is it? If not, what steps will you take to uncover this?

MIDPOINT ASSESSMENT

1. Thinking back to chapter one, how has your knowledge of the presence of God helped as you considered new leadership opportunities?

2. How have the shifting events in your community (chap. 2) enabled you to see areas where your gifts are needed?

3. How is your leadership platform shaping up (chap. 3)? Where do you see your strengths and passion taking you?

4. Have you completely surrendered all to God (chap. 4)? What new revelations has God brought forth since you surrendered?

CHAPTER SIX

THE PATH TO YOUR PLATFORM

Oh, that you would bless me and expand my territory!
Please be with me in all that I do,
and keep me from all trouble and pain!

1 Chronicles 4:10 (NLT)

HAVE YOU EVER WRESTLED with the following questions?

- What have I been put on earth to do?
- What am I passionate about?
- What is my circle of influence?

I certainly have. One of the allures of social media is that these outlets appeal to our intrinsic desire to understand and actualize our purpose in life. Many of us want to be lauded as significant. People create social media accounts like Instagram in the hope of gaining more and more followers—which is deemed by some as having significance.

Tom Peters wrote an article in August of 1997 titled "The Brand New You." Tom was one of the early voices who encouraged individuals to become their own brand. He wrote, "Regardless of age, regardless of position, regardless of the business we happen to be in, all of us need to understand the importance of branding. We are CEOs of our own companies: Me Inc. To be in business today, our most important job is to be head marketer for the brand called You."

The idea that our skills and gifts make us unique, marketable, and potentially profitable as an entrepreneur has revolutionized our culture. Social media has become the platform through which entrepreneurs promote their brand.

Yet a platform that transforms through effective leadership does so not through aesthetics like photoshopped images but through identity, character, authenticity, credibility, and influence. Platforms that are purposeful and powerful for kingdom impact are forged through revelation from God, introspection, adversity, healing, and restoration. Substance, not superficiality, is the goal.

So, how do we get there? The first step is to surrender to God, having discerned his will for our lives, and then following his process as he enables us to walk in the unique purpose he has called us to. Calling is directly tied to platform. Our platform is the vehicle by which others can witness how we steward the gifts God has given us as we serve him.

For many years I wrestled with understanding my purpose. Through Rick Warren's book *The Purpose Driven Life*, I first embarked on the process of unpacking what I felt passionate about in life. These discoveries lead me to postgraduate study, followed by my introduction to serving in ministry. But throughout this process, which culminated in 2017, I wrestled with God in prayer concerning my life's purpose. The concept of a platform was foreign to me. I never asked God for a platform. My desire was never to influence people. Instead, my desire was to please God. My platform emerged from a humble heart.

In our journey of faith, we might wrestle with the Lord for understanding. When our desire is to yield solely and wholly to God, we come to an understanding that missing his direction can take our life down paths and detours that rob us of precious time in fulfilling our purpose.

This reality births within us an intentional desire to be prayerful about seeking the plans of God. Wrestling with God means that we refuse to rely on our own understanding and instead accept that God *will* direct our path (Proverbs 3:5-6).

A man in the Bible literally wrestled with God and discovered his purpose.

MATTERS OF THE HEART

Before the death of his father Isaac, Jacob stole the patriarchal blessing, which was to be given to his brother Esau, by deceiving his father (Genesis 27:1-29). As a result, he had to run away from his homeland. But God passed on to Jacob the covenant he had previously made with Abraham (Genesis 28:1-4).

In Genesis 32, Jacob obeyed God's command to return to his own land and family but wanted protection from his brother Esau; Jacob thought Esau still hated him for stealing Esau's blessing. In this defining moment of hardship, Jacob reminded God of all that God had promised. If I were to paraphrase Jacob's thoughts at this point, they would go something like this: *I am in this place because I've obeyed you, so now I need you to deliver me from an enemy who wants to hinder your will from being accomplished in me* (Genesis 32:9-12). This was bold.

God responded by wrestling with Jacob. They wrestled all night until the break of dawn. But Jacob said he would not let go until he received God's blessing. What faith!

Jacob's new identity (Genesis 32:27-28) and the subsequent platform for his leadership was birthed because he first obeyed

God and then wrestled with God for the fulfillment of the Lord's will in his life.

This physical wrestling is symbolic of the spiritual wrestling match that sometimes takes place in the pursuit of God's purpose. During these wrestling matches Satan (or our own response to fear) causes a constant replay in our minds concerning our current condition. The goal is to cause us to doubt God and stop following his commands despite the fact that God is fulfilling his purposes in us.

With that in mind, we need to contend for our platform. We must make up our minds now that we will wrestle for its fulfillment.

Another example of the birthing of our platform is found in 2 Chronicles 1. Solomon, the son of King David, had taken control over the kingdom of Israel. God appeared to Solomon one night and invited him to ask of God whatever he wanted, with a promise that God would grant his request. Solomon asked for wisdom and knowledge to lead Israel according to God's will and purposes. The posture of Solomon's heart, driven by a humble desire to please God, incubated the presence of mind to respond to God in this way.

Pleased by Solomon's request, God promised to not only grant his request but also to give him what he didn't ask for—wealth and fame unparalleled by any other king before or after him. Why would God entrust Solomon with this? Solomon's heart had proven him trustworthy to govern from a position of stewardship rather than self-gratification. The posture of his heart brought forth influence and increase.

See God's pattern through these Scriptures? A godly platform is cultivated first in a heart rooted in obedience to Jesus Christ. It is then established through God's choices to use our lives and influence in the service of his kingdom. The motivation for our platform is not about finding significance in the eyes of others but living a life pleasing to the One who has given us purpose.

BIRTHING YOUR PLATFORM

In April 2017, I received an email forwarded by my then boss Mac Pier. The email had been sent to him by Cindy Bunch, the associate publisher of InterVarsity Press, who asked if I had any interest in writing a book. She wanted to meet me during the Q Conference, where I was scheduled to be a guest speaker.

I distinctly remember the night before I was to fly to Nashville, where Q was being hosted. I was heartbroken from a recent broken relationship and could not even muster the strength to pack. I called my mentor, Helen West. When she answered the phone, I sobbed and asked her to pray. I needed God to deliver me from the enemy who wanted to hinder God's will from being accomplished. She prayed, and as a result God flooded my heart with peace, enabling me to pack and go to Nashville. There, I met with Cindy and went on to speak before hundreds of leaders at Q. This book, which I began writing in 2018, is a product of that meeting. Sometimes a platform is birthed in a time of darkness. In those moments we may be humbled in a way that allows us to listen especially well to the whispers of the Spirit.

Within the course of one year, God had crystallized my understanding of the platform he was cultivating through me: to preach his Word, to teach and shepherd his flock, to write and share my voice with the world, to travel globally as an ambassador for God, connecting his people and mentoring the next generation of young leaders. These revelations had taken many years to manifest. It was as if the pieces of a puzzle were coming together, and the puzzle was God's original plan for my life. Yet I can't help but feel that more is waiting to be revealed.

Jada Pinkett Smith is an American actress, comedian, singer-songwriter, and businesswoman with a platform that's different from my own. In May of 2018, Jada, her mother, and her daughter started a web-based television show called *Red Table Talk*, which is broadcast on Facebook Watch. In each episode the trio, along with an invited guest, discuss various topics: loss, marriage, anxiety and depression, drug addiction, and so forth. The show became an overnight success, and as of August 2019 it boasted over 6.4 million Facebook followers.

Prior to launching *Red Table Talk*, Jada didn't have an Instagram account. However, she needed to market her personal brand, so in 2018 she created an Instagram account. In one year she had over two million followers. Jada has become known for possessing wisdom, great insight, and a voice of authenticity for her audience. Her personal brand has been accelerated because of her platform. Jada's example reveals that knowing our niche and the specific areas where we produce significant results can allow us to be purposeful in how our distinct passions are leveraged for maximum impact.

DAVID: SHEPHERDING A NATION

King David is described in the Scriptures as a man after God's own heart (1 Samuel 13:14). He was appointed as king over Israel after God had rejected Saul's kingship. David stewarded his platform as a valiant warrior and worshiper. Though he was anointed king as a youth (1 Samuel 16:11-13), decades passed before he ascended to the throne of Israel (2 Samuel 5). During the years he spent serving as Saul's armor bearer, first soothing an increasingly erratic Saul with music and then running from a jealous Saul, David depended on God. When he became king, he served as an example of godly kingship by accomplishing the purposes of God and not his own. He was passionate about the promises of God being fulfilled as Israel was purposed to defeat their enemies and possess the land God gave them to inherit. Even when David sinned, he publicly owned up to his wrongdoing (2 Samuel 12; Psalm 51). God rewarded David and the generations of his family to come.

God does not require perfection. Instead, he desires faithfulness anchored in obedience to his will and devotion to his lordship. How we leverage our platform as a vehicle for glorifying God determines the legacy we'll leave behind.

Remember, our yes to God has generational implications. We must carefully choose how we steward our platforms. Let's discuss how to do that.

BUILDING A PLATFORM

To build a platform our areas of impact and influence must be clear and in line with our spiritual gifts. We can start the process by answering this question: What are my unique and valuable attributes that systemically leave an impact in places God has called me to serve?

Part of the process of platform building is searching for recurring themes that speak to our uniqueness and the indelible mark God has called us to leave on this world. As some recurring themes come into focus, we consider how we might scale and amplify the impact of our voices to shine a light on these particular areas. The platform becomes the springboard for greater impact. It amplifies and legitimizes our message. Through a surrendered life to God, our platform takes on a kingdom agenda.

Building a platform is forged through identity, character, authenticity, credibility, and influence.

Integrity. I value people who demonstrate integrity in public and in private. They value integrity—doing what is right—over compromising to please people and gain popularity.

Susan Payne, an event planner, was candid with those who knew her well about her former struggles with theft and the fact that she had stolen hundreds of dollars from previous employers. When it came to events where she had to handle money, she would always have a cash-counting partner on hand to ensure she wasn't left alone with the money. No one asked Susan to take this step. Yet her previous mistakes caused her to place greater value on guarding herself against being a thief so she could be trusted.

In leadership we should be committed to stewarding our platform with integrity rather than bowing to the selfish interests of popularity. Popularity is fleeting—here today and gone tomorrow. But integrity builds a legacy.

Character. Character is determined by the standards that govern the way we live. "Bad company corrupts good character" (1 Corinthians 15:33). If your life is submitted to God and the authority of his Word, good character will be produced.

Character is cultivated in every decision we make. Do we come to work late and leave early? That's stealing company time. Do we take things that don't belong to us, thinking that someone else has an overabundance? That too is stealing. By our actions we're grooming our minds how to respond to similar situations. The bank robber didn't start off robbing banks but graduated to this level of criminality through a history of bad decision making. When we train ourselves to be godly in the small things, our character will prove itself in split-second decisions that could be life-changing; for example, posting on social media out of anger.

Today, we are all one sound bite away from being praised or vilified. People's lives and characters are daily being destroyed for seemingly ignorant and offensive responses to hot-button issues or comments taken out of context. We need to ask God to give us wisdom as we engage in social media.

Authenticity. There is such a demand for authentic leadership and honest and trustworthy voices. There are people with such credibility that they are regarded by enemies and foes alike as being fair, dependable, and authentic. In an article at Forbes.com, Kevin Kruse described authentic leaders as those who

- are self-aware and genuine.
- are mission driven and focused on results.
- lead with their heart.
- focus on the long-term.

Senator John McCain was an example of an authentic leader. The former prisoner of war was a US senator for thirty-one years and a candidate for the US presidency in 2008. Republicans and Democrats had great admiration and respect for Senator McCain. Such a profound display of bipartisanship could be seen at his funeral in 2018.

A significant moment that spoke volumes about Senator McCain's character occurred in 2008 when during a rally a woman told him she did not trust the Democratic nominee for president, Barack Obama, because he was an Arab. Although Obama was his opponent Senator McCain responded by telling the woman that she was wrong—Obama was not an Arab but an American and a decent man. McCain could have used that opportunity to feed the growing "birther controversy," a set of theories that asserted Obama was not born in the United States and subsequently was ineligible to run for president, but McCain chose not to denigrate another person. That's remarkable.

When we choose to operate in truth, we prove to people that we can be trusted to not intentionally deceive them. Whether they agree with us or not, at least they know where we stand. The truth sets us free (John 8:32)—a truth we can live by.

Credibility. How we treat people speaks volumes about our character and credibility. Actions communicate louder than anything we could ever say. The saying is true: people will always remember how we make them feel. According to an article by Peter Economy (the Leadership Guy), "Credible leaders walk the talk and make their actions speak louder than their words—they deliver what they promise. Leaders with established credibility are respected and trusted."

We want to intentionally foster credibility, which proclaims our life principles even when we're not present. Is this hard? No. It's intentional. This means valuing all the people we meet and not being a respecter of persons. God isn't (Acts 10:34)! I daily fight against becoming prideful while considering myself of lowly position. Be honest, even when we have to stand alone.

One of my personal mottos is that it is better to be righteous than right. Always yield to the will of the Lord. If vindication is required, let God fight our battles. This takes much faith and can be downright painful! But this posture is key to being anchored in "the peace of God, which transcends all understanding" (Philippians 4:7). A vengeful and unforgiving person is tormented by what was done and what was said. Be more concerned with honoring God in every matter. This doesn't mean we're striving for perfection; even when we are wrong, we must acknowledge it and try to make amends. Leave the rest to God.

Influence. A trend today, particularly for Instagram users, is to pay for social media followers. In a *Forbes* article Joresa Blount writes, "For a platform that's constantly changing its algorithm, it can sometimes seem impossible to truly start gaining traction." Many social media experts caution against doing so because of the oversaturation of fake accounts, which can lead to large numbers of fake followers. While the idea of a large audience may appeal to some, doing so will not gain godly influence.

Influence is the ability to steer the course of a person's life toward a meaningful outcome. In the case of a Christian, influence is our ability to point others toward the transformative power of Jesus Christ and encourage them to submit their lives daily to his lordship. Godly influence is levied by godly people. "Those who exalt themselves will be humbled, and those who humble themselves will be exalted" (Matthew 23:12 NLT). God grants influence to those whose integrity has been proven in private.

When I was in high school, a friend called me one night to tell me that she was pregnant. She didn't know what to do and sought me for guidance. She was contemplating having an abortion and had contacted me because I was someone who had an influence on her life.

I had a choice to make: I could encourage her to prayerfully explore the options involved in going through with the pregnancy (giving up her child for adoption or keeping the baby) or affirm her desire to abort. I regret to say that I chose the latter. I even provided her with the contact information for an abortion clinic.

Mercy, Lord! Think about how I used my influence. My friend went through with the abortion. Years later while in seminary, I took a course called "Treating the Post-Abortive Client." I searched for my friend on Facebook and was able to ask for her forgiveness. Through our exchange on Facebook, she told me she had forgiven me years before that. I was so grateful we could both find healing and peace.

During the semester when I took the course, I was leading the empowerment group for women at Bethel. I used this platform to invite postabortive women into an invitation-only group meeting to discuss their experiences. There we prayed for God's healing and deliverance.

Although a precious life had been lost, the knowledge I amassed in this area helped me to make sure the influence I had over other women was for good and not for evil.

How we influence others is critical in how we steward our platforms. In building a platform, we need to make our salvation and ministry the foundation—the substance of what God has called us to steward. We may not be called to establish a corporation or a faith-based company. But we can discern where God is leading us based on the places and frequency with which he's using our voice.

KEEP YOUR EYES ON GOD

As we build our platforms, we must be sure that God is promoting us rather than we promoting ourselves. We have to daily release the praises of others and redirect them to God, because any platform begins and ends with him.

Prayer and fasting are critical to discerning God's call as we steward our platforms. The Holy Spirit will then direct us.

In fall 2017, God directed me to find a personal assistant. I could sense that one day I would need one. I really wrestled with this because having an assistant might communicate self-importance to others. I'm also extremely private, and the idea of allowing access to the personal details of my life was scary.

God directed me to Essence Lee, who is an anointed youth leader at Bethel and has a tender heart but isn't a pushover. We didn't know each other well, yet I asked her if she would consider supporting me. Essence was immediately willing to help me and was honored that I asked. I didn't need help just yet, but I was so grateful to now have someone in mind I could call on in the future.

In fall 2018, Essence sought me out to remind me of our conversation and to let me know that she was available to help me free of charge. I labored with whether this was the right time to move forward with her as my assistant. Yet I had to acknowledge that her willingness at that time showed God's perfect timing because I would soon need an extra level of prayer and support that she was ready to give. God *sent* her to help me steward this platform that is yet to be actualized. I'm grateful for this season of favor and preparation. And, amazingly, as God's preparation affords us answers in advance of future needs, Essence would become my executive assistant. I've learned yet again to trust God with the platforms he's called me to.

REFLECTION QUESTIONS

1. How would you describe your platform? Write a paragraph in a journal describing it.

2. Who has affirmed this platform in your life?

3. How is God stretching your understanding of his will and purposes in your life?

4. Are you promoting yourself, or is God promoting you? How does your social media presence show this?

5. What steps are you taking toward cultivating identity, godly character, authenticity, credibility, and influence? Where are you struggling? Do you have an accountability partner in this area?

6. Do you sense God's leading to formalize your ministry platform into a corporate entity? If so, what steps will you take to do so?

CHAPTER SEVEN

LEADING IN THE CHURCH

God chose things despised by the world,
things counted as nothing at all, and used them
to bring to nothing what the world considers important.
As a result, no one can ever boast in the presence of God.

1 Corinthians 1:28-29 (NLT)

I AM A VERY LITERAL PERSON—always have been. My youngest sister, Faith, has told me that she is amused by the changing expressions on my face whenever she tells me a story that's meant to be a joke but I think it's a real-life event. She claims that my facial expressions change from shock to befuddlement to a partial acceptance, and then to the light bulb moment when I ask, "Wait a minute. Are you tricking me?"

Once, after a burst of hysterical laughter, she said, "You're so naive." But being wired to evaluate people, places, and things for what they present themselves to be has guarded me against being judgmental. I naturally see the promise in all things and believe the best until there is justifiable cause to embrace a different reality. This mindset has helped me to greatly value people, not just those who I think are similar to me.

But the naiveté was a detriment as I began working when I was thirteen—the legal age in New York State when youth can obtain working papers. My first job was as a nurse's assistant at the now closed St. Clare's Hospital in New York City. I worked in the clinic that served as the primary care location for inmates at the Bedford Hills Correctional Facility for Women. While I had the drive mentally and physically to work, emotionally I wasn't prepared to advocate for myself, maintain appropriate boundaries, address sexual harassment, or navigate crucial conversations with senior staff. When the inmates were in the clinic, due to my facing constant sexual harassment I would hide in the examination room. It was terrifying.

My mother stepped in to advocate for me with the hospital's human resources department when I faced challenging situations with my supervisor, who at times took advantage of my youth.

After that, I had many jobs at various hospitals, financial institutions, schools, and corporations. I met a lot of people and experienced different work cultures and management styles, which helped me discern the environments I should and shouldn't work in.

Because I had worked in the secular arena, I didn't have a frame of reference for working in the church. My concept of church emerged from the Sunday morning worship experiences I'd attended. In my young adult years my hunger for God was the lens I viewed the church through—as my connection place to the Lord, my source for healing and renewal. I experienced the euphoria of worship and the empowering exegesis (interpretation) of Scripture, which radically changed my life. I had such admiration for ministers who served on Sundays—their passion for God, giftedness, and compassion for the people. Many of them displayed confidence I deeply admired and desired for myself. In the church I found safety from a world outside the doors of the church that was not as kind. Within the church, however, I discovered a new paradigm.

PARADIGM SHIFT

Jesus was an emerging leader who constantly defied social conventions. His public ministry encompassed a three-year period in which he not only empowered Jewish males in their early thirties but also revolutionized generations with the power of God's Word—those with "ears to hear" (Matthew 11:15). Jesus was sent as an offering to the world but was received only by a few. Although being rejected was part of his journey, Christ thrived in the midst of rejection because he understood the role he was called to play. Knowing his role enabled him to weather the storms of being misunderstood and rejected.

Apart from studying Jesus' life, I expected work in the church to be euphoric: constant joy, worship, and thanksgiving all day long; a source of shelter and safety; a reprieve from a cold world. In many ways my view of the church directly paralleled how I thought of heaven.

At the Last Supper, Jesus, after breaking bread and taking the cup of wine along with his disciples and giving thanks to God for the coming of a new covenant, spoke to the reality that one of them would betray him, for it had *already been determined* by God that Jesus must die (Luke 22:7-22). The concept that while living out God's predetermined will for my life I too might experience betrayal, deception, falsehoods spoken against me and my character, and be dealt with harshly at times by people I admired was one of the hardest realities I've had to accept and endure.

I expected people to love each other in spite of their faults and shortcomings, give people the benefit of the doubt, take ownership of how our worldview might skew our perceptions, and with great diligence and care preserve the integrity of fellowship. But this is not always the reality. We are flawed, broken sinners saved by the grace of God. If I was going to survive in the church, I had to shift lest I join the throngs of hurting people who have seen the clay feet of other believers and turned completely away from God.

I had to acknowledge my naiveté. I was looking toward external sources to grant me a sense of stability, affirmation, peace, and protection, all without accepting that while we can attain a measure of this in our relationship with others, we will experience many trials and tribulations in this life. But there is a promise: we can be of good cheer because Jesus has overcome the world (John 16:33). I needed to overcome mentally and emotionally. I needed to trust that no matter what I endured, the promise of resurrection in every situation was possible.

I QUIT!

Through my work at Movement.org I was introduced to the ministry of Pete Scazzero, the founding pastor of New Life Fellowship Church in Queens. He's the author of *Emotionally Healthy Spiritually*, and he was an instructor at Movement.org's Advance Leadership Intensive. Peter's wife, Geri, wrote a book titled *I Quit: Stop Pretending Everything Is Fine and Change Your Life*, which changed my life! It is a radical book that told the story of when Geri actually stopped attending their church. She writes,

> The kind of quitting I'm talking about isn't about weakness or giving up in despair. It is about strength and choosing to live in the truth. This requires the death of illusions. It means ceasing to pretend that everything is fine when it's not. . . . When we quit those things, which are damaging to our souls or the souls of others, we are freed up to choose other ways of being and relating that are rooted in love and lead to life.

This book helped me to acknowledge that I had some gaping wounds that still needed healing, and it was okay to say this. I wasn't sure of my future or God's plans for me. I didn't have a sense of how all of the events in my life might lead toward a greater good. I felt that I needed someone to say, "Ebony, you're okay! Ebony, I see great value in you! Ebony, your past has not obliterated your hopes and dreams for your future."

I remember during the height of some terse exchanges I had with a former friend she said I was a weak person who needed to be stroked. Yeah, her words stung. I know now she was hurting and was lashing out, but I wrestled for some time with what she said. *Was I weak?* I thank God for caring people in my life who helped me understand that I was not weak at all. They helped me to acknowledge that I was on the mend from the pain of many life experiences. Sometimes pain can hinder our ability to live in the fullness of God's truth that we are "fearfully and wonderfully made" (Psalm 139:14).

As a lay leader I approached people with what I'd hoped they'd fulfill in me versus what God had intended those relationships to be. For example, I would say yes to almost every task no matter what my passion for the project happened to be: I wanted affirmation, wanted to be liked. And I would say what I thought someone wanted to hear rather than what I knew to be true because I feared what others thought of me. I wanted to know that I was okay.

Until I found the strength to quit pretending I was okay emotionally, I suffered terribly for many years. There wasn't a specific sermon I heard preached that led to this deeper self-evaluation—I simply was tired. Tired of hurting, tired of not protecting myself. Tired of pretending. Simply tired of me!

Many of us are in the same boat. A culture of dishonesty can breed bitterness and resentment of others in our lives. We won't be able to effectively lead others when being authentic is a challenge. Emotional health is an essential component of leadership. If we don't address our souls' ache for healing, we will derail our ability to lead effectively.

God knew I needed to read Geri's book in order to address the reality of my own situation. Geri had to quit people pleasing, quit the avoidance of maintaining healthy boundaries, and being dishonest in communicating how she felt. I needed to wrestle with some deep inadequacies or I would never rise to the level of emotional maturity that effective leadership requires. I'd never survive in a world that continually sought to invalidate my existence as an African American, as a woman, and as a woman called to preach and teach.

Geri returned to New Life Fellowship Church with a commitment to care for her soul and the souls of others by observing biblical truth, and I returned to my own life with the same intention. But in doing so I needed to understand a deeper truth.

WHO DOES GOD SAY I AM?

My local church affirms women in ministry. Women serve as ministry leaders, preachers, and executive or associate pastors. That's rare. I didn't know how rare this is until I began working for a parachurch organization.

According to the 2012 National Congregations Study, roughly 11 percent of congregations had a woman serving in a senior leadership role or as the sole pastor of a church. There are denominations that presently do not ordain women or allow them to lead congregations. This was another blow to my thinking that in the church I would find widespread affirmation as a woman in leadership.

In Matthew 16:13-16, we encounter Jesus in conversation with Peter:

> When Jesus came to the region of Caesarea Philippi, he asked his disciples, "Who do people say the Son of Man is?"
>
> They replied, "Some say John the Baptist; others say Elijah; and still others, Jeremiah or one of the prophets."
>
> "But what about you?" he asked. "Who do you say I am?"
>
> Simon Peter answered, "You are the Messiah, the Son of the living God."

Jesus went on to tell Peter that flesh and blood could not have revealed this truth to Peter. Only the Holy Spirit could have revealed this. This passage has become an anchor in my life. The Holy Spirit affirmed within me first that I have been called to preach the gospel, which was later confirmed by others.

When people judge us through the lens of their experience and sometimes through their flawed understanding of Scripture, it is essential to hold on to the truth of who we are and what God has called us to do. Often God's affirmation will have to be enough.

Many people base their theology that women should not preach on 1 Corinthians 14:34-35: "Women should be silent during the church meetings. It is not proper for them to speak. They should be submissive, just as the law says. If they have any questions, they should ask their husbands at home, for it is improper for women to speak in church meetings" (NLT).

But consider the context. Here the apostle Paul is attempting to restore order in the Corinthian congregation, which was struggling to find stability. This does not mean that all women for all time should be silent. After all, the Bible has many accounts of Jesus empowering women to share their faith.

In John 4, Jesus encountered a Samaritan woman while sitting at the well of Jacob. What he told this woman about herself—that she'd had five husbands and was with a man who was not her husband—pierced her heart. But he didn't condemn her as her culture undoubtedly did. He offered her water that would forever quench a thirst she didn't know she had. Water, which typifies the Holy Spirit here, indicates that Jesus offered to quench her thirst for forgiveness, healing, reconciliation, salvation, deliverance, and redemption.

This was an encounter at a well named for Jacob, who wrestled with the angel of the Lord. It appears that through Jesus' encounter with this woman at Jacob's well God was wrestling with every system that judged the Samaritan woman's existence and was liberating her to walk in a new identity.

When the disciples returned to the well, they were "shocked to find him talking to a woman" (John 4:27 NLT). Clearly, they didn't think Jesus would be ministering to her. Yet the woman didn't question why Jesus would favor her in this way; instead, she ran to town to tell others what he had done for her.

Likewise, I've endeavored to stand as a woman preacher and leader in the midst of a culture where some male pastors refuse to reference me as "Pastor" or "Reverend" but only as "Sister Ebony" or "Minister Ebony" when introducing me to other men. This distinction is never explained. Yet, I've *never* heard these same leaders call a male elder or pastor "Brother So-and-so."

There have been other challenges. In 2015, I attended a partner meeting for Movement.org and overheard someone say that a planned prayer event had a predominately male roster; only one woman was scheduled to speak. I heard someone say, "You should ask Ebony." And within hours I was invited to speak at the event. I shared with the pastor that I welcomed the opportunity to participate, but only if the invitation was not due to my race, age, and gender. I felt I could operate at this level of transparency and would be understood.

The pastor assured me that race, age, and gender were not reasons for the invitation and that he regarded me in the same manner as the other program speakers. I accepted the invitation.

As the event drew nearer the pastor's assistant communicated that my speaking time had been reduced due to program constraints, which was totally fine with me. As an events manager I understood the need to make adjustments to a speaker's time. Then I received another email from the assistant that I was now asked to share my speaking time with one of the event sponsors and that I would no longer be speaking but instead was invited to pray a scripted prayer that the sponsor had prepared.

I was taken aback. My image had been widely circulated as part of the event's promotion in print form and on social media.

Although I had not been honored by the event organizer, I still showed up to the event and prayed. The event program had not been updated in time. I was still listed as a speaker with note pages included for the talk I never gave. Throughout the event people kept looking at me, wondering when I would speak. It was one of my most embarrassing experiences. Though the event organizer never apologized, I forgave him and let it go.

As I left the event that night, I encountered a co-laborer in ministry who lamented that she wished there were more women in the program. I did my best to encourage her. I could see how exasperated she felt. I never shared my experience with her. My goal was to avoid shaming the pastor or the ministry.

A year or so later the same pastor asked me to participate in a video project to endorse an evangelistic outreach being held in New York City later that year. Although I was sick and his crew was filming the video within the hour, I agreed to help him. I filmed my endorsement in less than ten minutes and continued on with my day. A few months later I watched the promo for the event. Wouldn't you know it—I was not included. I asked him what happened this time. He flailed his arms and lamented how he had no control over the final cut that his team edited, blah, blah, blah! The final footage showed all male endorsers.

There's a saying: Fool me once, shame on you; fool me twice, shame on me.

My female friends in ministry and I have shared countless war stories of devaluing experiences we've had as women in ministry and the blatant disrespect of God's affirmation of his presence in our lives. The Ebony I used to be could not have survived in this world where men and women believe that women shouldn't lead or preach. God could never trust what I'd say or do if I didn't embrace his affirmation of calling in my life.

No matter our race, gender, or age, we will encounter those who will judge our call to the position we are in, even in the church. We can attempt to justify our position or direct them to take their complaints to God. Either way, their opinions are not our burden to carry. When necessary, it might be valuable to have a frank conversation with a person we perceive as judging us.

CONFRONT TRUTH

I have been disappointed by how many church leaders avoid having crucial conversations as if they were the bubonic plague. Instead, they believe the innuendos, reasoning, and deductions they've never investigated but have received as factual, allowing them to shape the way they view others. This, of course, limits the depth of their personal relationships. It's mind boggling. Having a conversation takes much less energy!

I've watched senior leaders allow leaders under their purview to mistreat others who then hope *someone else* will confront that leader about this hurtful behavior. The culture of an organization or church will be as healthy as the senior leader allows it to be. In an unhealthy and fractured culture, we'll find rampant discord and lack of trust. Having crucial conversations is a way of guarding against the schemes of the enemy and preventing the little foxes from spoiling the vine (Song of Songs 2:15).

Effective leadership requires great courage. A fractured leadership culture leaves in its wake a trail of wounded people and broken relationships. To counter this we must learn the value of confronting rather than believing hearsay and every thought that enters our minds. We need to courageously confront the truth in ourselves and others and accept that we are not always right—we misjudge situations often because we view current realities through the lens of a flawed and broken past. Conversations help us to not work overtime trying to figure out why someone did or said something. Just ask that person!

In her book *Fierce Conversations* Susan Scott writes,

> All confrontation is a search for truth. Who owns the truth? Each of us owns a piece of it, and nobody owns all of it. Let us keep in mind that confrontation is a conversation. As with all fierce conversations, the four purposes of a confrontation are to: interrogate reality, provoke learning, tackle tough challenges and enrich relationships.

Before engaging in a fierce conversation, we have to be open to the reality that we might have been mistaken in our initial understanding of an issue. Searching for truth will require us to analyze objectively and critically, knowing that the enemy desires no resolution *and* severed relationships. Our position in the conversation is that God has the power to redeem all things, even misunderstandings. Our goal is truth, learning, and understanding.

Those who identify as leaders have to get used to having fierce conversations. The people we lead will thank us for creating a healthy and safe culture where abuse and mistreatment of others are confronted and not tolerated. When we do, we'll experience longevity of service and greater productivity within our team. Our decision about whether or not to have a fierce conversation shouldn't depend on how the other person might respond.

Without fierce conversations our ability to preserve the integrity of our relationships will be hindered. So, when we recognize that change must take place, we don't hope for *others* to do what needs to be done. We just do it!

NONE OF US HAS ARRIVED

"God opposes the proud but shows favor to the humble" (James 4:6). Effective leaders are committed to lifelong learning. While seminary education is valuable for those who feel called to ministry, serving God doesn't require a degree or certification—just a willing heart. But as we administer our duties of leadership, wanting to learn from others who've traveled the road we're undertaking is natural. Adding tools to our toolbox and keeping up with the changing needs of people and culture will serve us well as we lead people, teams, and organizations. Everybody wins when a leader gets better.

To aid my leadership development I attend conferences. For the past eight years I have attended the Willow Creek Association's Global Leadership Summit (GLS), a two-day program offering leadership development sessions from some of today's best thought leaders. I have also attended the Growth Skills Foundation Ultimate Leadership Intensive with Henry Cloud and John Townsend. I arrived at the training with an open heart, not knowing what to expect. I was blown away by the teaching and the time allotted for processing and application, which uncovered areas of my emotional health and professional development I am committed to improving on.

As part of the intensive I was reminded about the value of accountability partners. Shortly after the training one of my accountability partners called to find out how I was tracking with one of my goals. I appreciated her remembering and was happy to report that I had made some improvements.

Accountability partners help us manage our blind spots. They should be people we trust whose intentions toward us are clear. They will not stroke us when we're wrong but instead will confront us with the truth. These are people we feel free to be transparent with, even when we are suffering. Those who are mentoring us make good accountability partners. So do individuals who are operating at the same level of leadership as we are and have a similar life experience. I have five accountability partners; I know I can find safety, truth, and trust with each.

I have a library in my home full of books from seminary, work, and ministry. The number of resources that can make us more effective in leadership is endless. The choice to be better is ours. I hope each of us will commit to continual spiritual, emotional, and mental replenishment. We should make a yearly appointment on our calendars and set a goal for the number of books we'd like to read per quarter. It might be good to invite our leadership team to join us. I've never met a person who didn't value this kind of investment.

IT DOES TAKE ALL THAT

Effective leadership requires great intentionality. Leadership is not easy; it is a call that must be answered and handled with great responsibility. In most cases the leaders who made the greatest impact on us are those who affirmed us, valued our work, invested in us, pushed us toward goals we never thought attainable, and uncovered gifts and talents we didn't know we had. They may have been gifted to serve us in these ways. I can guarantee they felt called to invest in leaders like us and sought out opportunities to do so. There is a generation of people needing us to do the same.

A large part of my leadership is seeking to represent the type of leadership I wish I had had. I want to be better for those I serve alongside. I hope I'll create far more meaningful experiences for them than some leaders offered to me. In my presence I want those I lead and serve to know I value and support them, that I'm committed to their success, and that it is an honor to have them in my life.

This is what Jesus did. He affirmed, redeemed, and empowered everyday people everywhere he traveled. We are invited to do the same.

REFLECTION QUESTIONS

1. What, if anything, have you discerned within your ministry that needs a paradigm shift?

2. How are you handling the brokenness of people and the ways they have failed you?

3. Have you experienced judgment or discrimination due to your race, gender, or age? How are you confronting the effect of this in your life?

4. Where are you intentionally confronting the truth?

5. How comfortable are you with having fierce conversations? Explain.

6. What's your growth plan this year? Where will you go to be invested in?

7. Do you have accountability partners? If yes, how often are you engaging them?

CHAPTER EIGHT

LEADING IN THE MARKETPLACE

Whatever you do, work at it with all your heart,
as working for the Lord, not for human masters,
since you know that you will receive an inheritance from
the Lord as a reward. It is the Lord Christ you are serving.

COLOSSIANS 3:23-24

SUCCESSFUL AND EFFECTIVE LEADERSHIP is as much about our understanding of the type of leader we want to be and our commitment to developing into that kind of leader as it is about any position we desire to have.

My leadership identity was shaped by my cultural identity. Since college I've studied and worked in environments where I was either one of a handful or the only African American or the only woman. I encountered people from different ethnicities who previously had not had much contact with the African American experience. So I became the lens through which they viewed African Americans. I would field questions about where I lived, past jobs or education, my family, and even my hair and how long certain styles took to configure. These questions often came across as if I were on display—an object being marveled at—rather than as a real attempt to get to know me.

I received compliments about how articulate or poised I was, but the underlying sentiment was that I was the exception and not the norm, that my presence and my character dispelled stereotypes some believed as they wrestled with the identity of the woman before them.

How I presented myself in these spaces was largely driven by my desire to never fill stereotypes. I wanted to show those with prejudiced views that it is never okay to judge (Matthew 7:1). I was driven to be well-informed so I could contribute to all conversations around me. This drive made me resourceful. I wanted to look the part, dressing professionally and keeping my love for neon-colored fingernails to a minimum. Ha! I did so because I refused to be boxed into what the twenty-four-hour news cycle says about minorities.

KNOW YOURSELF

Carla Ann Harris is the author of *Strategize to Win* and vice chairman, managing director, and senior client adviser at Morgan Stanley. I've admired her as a strong African American female business leader.

In 2018, Carla was a speaker at Willow Creek Association's Global Leadership Summit. During her talk she spoke about learning to bring her whole self to business meetings and to any other place she was called. Bringing her *whole self* meant she didn't leave any part of her identity outside of the room in order to fit inside of the room. She was Carla of the Catholic faith, the opera singer, author, and businesswoman.

Her words liberated me to follow suit. I did not have to carry the weight of having to be a model African American woman in order to avoid being judged because of my race before I had the opportunity to display my character. I am Ebony the Christian, pastor, sports enthusiast, world traveler, and intercessor; someone who loves to entertain and who is fun, loving, giving, and loyal. I like fried chicken, collard greens, and other types of soul food! But I also love sushi, raw oysters and clams, crudités, and so on.

In *Strategize to Win* Carla writes, "One of the most important facets of positioning yourself for success is to be self-aware. You must know who you are and who you aspire to be. I find that many professionals do not proceed successfully in their careers because they are not aware of who they really are." Marketplace leader, know thyself!

THE SERVANT

For the past eight years I've worked for parachurch organizations. *Para*, in the Greek language, means to "come alongside." The role of parachurch organizations is to come alongside local churches and provide the ministries these churches could not support alone.

One of the biggest contrasts to working in a faith-based environment was the concept of teamwork. In my previous roles with nonprofit organizations, my performance evaluation was based on my ability to meet and exceed the expectations of my role. In these organizations we were neither expected to help other staff complete their work or lend staff support interdepartmentally nor evaluated along those lines. The culture could be categorized as "sink or swim." I discovered a concept of teamwork foreign to me, and I had to quickly adapt, serving others through my work became more of my focus. The gift of exercising this skill set led to greater personal fulfillment for me with opportunities to develop other leaders. These skills led to promotions from managerial to director-level positions.

Culture dictates the type of leadership required. Leadership is an act of service whether we work for faith-based organizations or not. If we are servants of God, where we work is the outflow of that service. God has sent us to that ministry, company, or organization to serve the entity's mission and ideals, as well as serving our staff and colleagues. When service is our posture, our leadership can be more of an accelerant than a hindrance. There's no "I" in team.

In his book *The Ideal Team Player* Patrick Lencioni mentions that the three essential virtues of a team player are humility, hunger, and people smarts, with humility being the most important of the three. Lencioni writes, "In the context of teamwork, humility is largely what it seems to be. Great team players lack excessive ego or concerns about status. They are quick to point out the contributions of others and slow to seek attention for their own."

According to Lencioni, two types of people who lack humility are the overly arrogant and those who lack self-confidence. The arrogant magnify their individual contributions to a project over the success of the team. Their focus is self-aggrandizement and feeding into the platform they seek for themselves. Those who lack self-confidence don't bring their whole selves—all of their gifts, talents, and abilities—to the team. The Bible says, "The eye cannot say to the hand, 'I don't need you!' And the head cannot say to the feet, 'I don't need you!'" (1 Corinthians 12:21). We cannot place more value on one team member over the other. When we encounter someone who lacks self-confidence, our job is to mine the treasure within that person so that the team's collective work is enriched.

Teams function well when we have the "right people on the bus," as Jim Collins describes in his book *Good to Great*. Churches, companies, and organizations have the capacity to transition from *good* to *great* when Level 5 leaders are present. Like Lencioni, Collins would agree that humility is one of the best attributes of Level 5 leaders. Collins writes, "Self-effacing, quiet, reserved, even shy—these leaders are a paradoxical blend of personal humility and professional will. They are more like Lincoln and Socrates than Patton or Caesar." I am a Level 5 leader and am grateful for the work of Collins to affirm the value of my personality and leadership blend.

At one point in my career I was convinced that my introversion was negative. I was chided for not speaking up in meetings by those who felt I had not yet *found* my voice. The pressure was great! However, I couldn't help that my best thinking was done in solitude. I needed time to process the information I had received. Yet, because I was constantly being judged for my performance in meetings, I had to push myself to offer feedback in meetings.

When we are silent, people may assume that we have nothing to say or that our presence doesn't add value. If we're introverted, we'll have to guard against this. There may be times when we're unfairly judged. The evil vices of jealousy and envy can and will manifest in the marketplace. If we are believers, when we sense that we've been plunged into hard circumstances that restrict our advancement, we need to seek God. A Scripture that comforts me and that I've boldly declared to God many times in prayer is, "The battle is not yours, but God's" (2 Chronicles 20:15).

Joseph, in the book of Genesis, experienced this firsthand when jealousy plunged him into a bad situation that God used to bring about a good outcome.

THE PURPOSE IN PAIN

Most people have heard the story of Joseph and his eleven brothers. They were the sons of Jacob. Joseph's mother was Rachel, Jacob's favorite wife (Genesis 29:30). Because of this,

Joseph's father loved him more than the rest of his sons and showed that love by making a special robe for him, which caused Joseph's brothers to hate him. And when Joseph shared two dreams in which his brothers seemed to bow down to him, they hated him all the more.

One day as Joseph's brothers were grazing their father's flock near Shechem, Joseph was sent by their father to check on them. After learning of Joseph's arrival, the brothers plotted to kill him. But Reuben, the oldest, pleaded with his brothers to instead throw Joseph into a cistern, intending to later return for Joseph. But Judah had another idea: sell Joseph to Ishmaelite merchants headed for Egypt. Joseph was sold for twenty shekels (Genesis 37).

Joseph eventually became a slave to Potiphar, one of Pharaoh's officials. God was with Joseph and prospered him in everything he did (Genesis 39). But when Potiphar's wife attempted to seduce Joseph and he refused her advances, Joseph was thrown into prison. There, God enabled Joseph to interpret the dreams of two fellow prisoners, Pharaoh's chief baker and chief cupbearer. The chief cupbearer's dream was fulfilled, but when he was restored to his place of service, he forgot about Joseph until two years later when Pharaoh had two dreams he didn't understand. God had positioned Joseph to find favor with Pharaoh (Genesis 41).

After Joseph interpreted Pharaoh's dreams, predicting years of abundance followed by years of famine, Joseph's skill and wisdom caused Pharaoh to promote Joseph to a position of authority.

The famine affected not only the Egyptians but other nations as well. Joseph's family was forced to travel to Egypt for food (Genesis 42). Joseph, now governor in Egypt, had a choice: give food to his brothers or take revenge. Joseph chose the latter. His statements to his brothers have forever shaped how I view adversity and the people God uses in my trials:

Do not be distressed and do not be angry with yourselves for selling me here, because it was to save lives that God sent me ahead of you. For two years now there has been famine in the land, and for the next five years there will be no plowing and reaping. But God sent me ahead of you to preserve for you a remnant on earth and to save your lives by a great deliverance. (Genesis 45:5-7)

After the death of their father Joseph sought to reassure his brothers of his forgiveness: "Am I God, that I can punish you? You intended to harm me, but God intended it all for good" (Genesis 50:19-20 NLT).

It might be hard to believe, but God orchestrated this entire chain of events to save the lives of Joseph and his family. Sometimes it is hard for us to accept that the God of mercy, love, and grace would use pain, rejection, and despair to position us for promotion, but he does.

When we submit to God's sovereignty, we can accept that enduring hardship is a necessary part of leadership training. Hardship will refine our ideals, sharpen our gifts, uncover new talents, and remind us and others that God's presence is with us.

Proverbs 21:1 says, "The king's heart is like a stream of water directed by the LORD; he guides it wherever he pleases" (NLT). God will turn the heart of anyone in the direction he needs it to go to accomplish his will in our lives, families, communities, jobs, cities, nation, and world. Before we lament what people have done to us and the very difficult experiences we've endured, we might ask God for his purpose behind the pain. We ask him to help us exercise wisdom in how to navigate our relationships with people and what boundaries we might need to erect to guard our hearts. But understand that the perfection of our leadership gifts has been charged to the Lord.

Adversity is hard. When we're going through painful experiences, God's plan seems so far off. And if God had asked us to endure hardship to get to where he was taking us, we might have declined to follow his plan.

I want to encourage everyone to hold on. There is purpose in our pain. God has the uncanny ability to redeem time and turn our mess into our message. Submit to his process. Go *through* the journey, but don't get stuck on what *they* did or said. They are a tool in the hands of God. We've been called to a greater purpose. Leaders lead, and we will lead others out of the same experiences we've endured.

DARE TO SERVE

Joseph embodied the message of Colossians 3:23-24: "Whatever you do, work at it with all your heart, as working for the Lord, not for human masters, since you know that you will receive an inheritance from the Lord as a reward." Daring to serve others, no matter what our condition happens to be, helps us to remember *God is in control. God is sovereign. I am not destitute in this place. I am never alone.* If we're driven this way, we will have the posture of a servant, whether we work for a ministry or a business. "The earth is the LORD's, and everything in it" (Psalm 24:1).

Cheryl Bachelder, the former CEO of Popeyes Louisiana Kitchen, believes that "if you move yourself out of the spotlight and dare to serve others, you will deliver superior results." Joseph delivered superior results because he dared to serve. This model of excellent and effective leadership differs from what most people think leadership is—accolades and living in the spotlight. Level 5 leaders don't want the spotlight. Humble leaders will resist it at every turn. The win for these great leaders is this: we delivered, we out performed, we made leaders better, and we left a lasting legacy that no one can erase.

Leaders help people move from one place to another. They drive teams toward what Bachelder calls a "daring destination," the point of superior results. As leaders, we want to help individuals and teams define the following:

- What does success look like?
- How will we get to the destination we want to reach?
- Who do we need as part of our team to get there?
- What roadblocks are we facing?
- What solutions will help us reach our goals?

Effective leaders have a vision for where they want to take those they lead, and they define the goals they want to accomplish together. Coaches for sports teams convey the goals for the season in training camp, not mid-season. Their goal is to create buy-in at the outset. When a team buys into their leader's vision, they follow it. It is also important to acknowledge what changes need to be made to eliminate hindrances to success from the beginning. The team has to perceive the destination in order to believe it is attainable. A zero wins, sixteen losses football team will not buy into the vision that they will win the Super Bowl next season if the organization and coaching staff does not address the factors and personnel that contributed to a culture of loss.

As we make changes and see results, we have to be intentional about celebrating successes on the road to accomplishing the daring destination. Then the team's confidence that the plan they've submitted to is working.

As I read *Dare to Serve* and other leadership books, I was surprised by the way biblical principles of humility and service are widely accepted as traits of great leaders. I realized that among some Christians the principles of the Bible aren't seen as transferable outside of the church. But Jesus never erected a barrier between sacred and secular. He modeled how God's Word is interchangeable, relevant, and powerful for the whole world.

My primary focus is on the development of the leadership gifts of others within their spheres of influence. That is a kingdom agenda. As a church and marketplace leader, I don't discourage Christians from being athletes, artists, business professionals, entertainers, fashion designers. I say go for it! Bring your whole God-loving self to the table. Be a great leader and demonstrate the power of God in so doing.

In 2019, I began mentoring a group of fourteen emerging marketplace leaders. God had stirred this desire in my heart since the summer of 2018. I always feel time poor, so when to do this was daunting. Since God was leading me, however, I knew I had to be intentional about making time. We decided to meet once per quarter, four hours each time. I gave everyone the assignment to craft a personal statement and a mission statement. When we know our purpose as leaders, we'll choose where to lend our time, talents, and treasure based on our callings and not simply our abilities.

My personal statement is this: *To lead, empower, and equip a generation of believers who will advance God's kingdom in the spheres of influence where they've been planted.* My mission statement is this: *To shine light in darkness, surrendering all to God and courageously following Christ.* Our personal statements and mission statements should be clear, distinct, short, and memorable. Knowing our personal purpose will help us to decipher what matters most and provide a constant source of affirmation and encouragement as we invest our time, talent, and treasure in people and our work. I want to do what matters most. I want to make the most of every opportunity before me.

MOVING UP!

In 2015, I was working at Movement.org as the director of Movement Day and Events. I had been planning, managing, and now directing since I graduated from college. Yet I was beginning to question my next vocational move. I was experiencing an awakening and desired to grow in new areas and discover my purpose. I was passionate about Jesus, but my passion for my work was not at the same level. The more I served alongside younger leaders at my local church through our Third Service auxiliary ministry, the more I realized how much I loved working with them. They gave me life, joy, and excitement. Their love for me was real and tangible. I saw the investment I had made in their lives and they had made in mine. Working with them became the best part of serving in ministry.

As work intensified for me due to plans my team and I were making to host three thousand leaders from ninety-five countries for Movement Day Global Cities at the Jacob Javits Convention Center in New York City, my life became consumed with leading our team in executing this week-long gathering. It was by far the largest and most multifaceted event I'd ever directed. My team and I worked the hardest we ever had, and it was an incredible gathering that has had a lasting effect globally with the launch of Movement Day Expressions (MDE) across five continents.

In 2017, I was promoted into a new role for the organization as director of Movement Day Expressions. I began consulting with and coaching city leaders globally who wanted to launch an expression of Movement Day. I had never coached leaders this way before, but I was willing to learn and grow. The organization was expanding and diversifying, and I wanted to help lead us in the changes ahead. So, I centered the staff's strategic planning on what success for MDE would look like. It was hard to measure.

Success was not up to our team; success would now be defined by the adopters of Movement Day.

Although I wrestled internally with my next steps professionally, God was opening incredible doors for me as a network leader, an ambassador of MDE globally, and through speaking engagements. It was an exciting and rewarding time, yet I knew something on the other side of all this had not yet been revealed.

In June 2017, I began to sense a major life transition was ahead for me. I had been in a weekly rhythm of fasting and prayer to know God's will for my future, and increasingly a theme of change resonated within me. I agreed with what God put in my heart, and when appropriate I started sharing with others that I sensed a major life change was ahead and I was waiting for its manifestation.

During this time I was invited by Mac Pier to take his seat on the board of the Mission America Coalition (MAC) as he transitioned off. I didn't know much about MAC, but I knew the legacy of its leaders and history. I was honored and felt it was a good next step for me. After I joined the board, there was a transition in leadership with Nick Hall assuming the role of president. I'd heard Nick speak at a Concerts of Prayer Greater New York Pastors' Prayer Summit in either 2012 or 2013. We hadn't been introduced personally, but I remembered his clear passion for God.

The Mission America Coalition was rebranded in 2018 and renamed The Table Coalition (TTC). As TTC was rebranding, Nick invited me into conversations about what the renewed missional focus of the organization could look like. Nick also invited me to be guest speaker at TTC's National Gathering in October 2018 and also to share my testimony of reconciliation and forgiveness with my dad at PULSE Movement's Together evangelistic outreach at the Texas Motor Speedway later that month. PULSE's mission is to awaken culture to the reality of Jesus.

At Together, hundreds of thousands participated in one of the most powerful outreaches I'd ever witnessed. I was struck by the vision, hunger, and fervor to serve this next generation and wanted to be a part of this growing work.

MY NEXT

As I reflected on my time at the TTC National Gathering and Together, I intentionally sought God in fasting and prayer concerning all I was sensing and my desire for my life to be devoted to living out my passion, which I now identified as discipling the next generation. I had to acknowledge that the drive for my work at Movement.org was waning. I saw a tremendous opportunity for MDE's growth on the horizon, but I knew intuitively that I didn't have the drive to take it there because I didn't have the vision or the energy for it.

When our identity is not tied to our work but instead is tied to Christ, we won't hold onto a position just because we found success in the role. Instead, our heart will be for the mission of the organization to be accelerated whether through us or someone else. It's important to recognize when our vision and passion for our work have waned. It could mean that we have outgrown a seat on the bus. We want to guard against becoming complacent, capping our continued professional growth and impeding the progress of others.

Sometime thereafter, Nick invited me to consider joining PULSE's staff. I marveled at Nick's passion, vision, and leadership, and had grown to value his friendship. While I was honored by his invitation and was open to exploring the possibilities, I didn't feel ready to go deeper into those conversations. I wanted to transition into my next opportunity vocationally, but I wasn't sure when, where, and how.

As I was talking to the Lord about all I was feeling, I heard God ask me, *What are you afraid of?* I was stunned by his question. I didn't realize I was afraid. With that question, I stepped back to prayerfully consider Nick's invitation. Was his invitation part of the major life change I was expecting? Was PULSE where God was sending me next? I weighed this opportunity against my purpose, my mission, and my passion.

I love young people. I love to mentor, strategize, and develop new initiatives. Working at PULSE would encompass these opportunities. The more I settled into the idea that it was okay for me to transition from a job and ministry team that I had served with for eight years, the more my excitement for my next position grew. I decided to put fear aside and walk toward my next daring destination.

I resigned from my role at Movement.org and assumed the role of vice president of multiplication at PULSE in June 2019. As God would have it, I get to serve the directors of the Table Coalition and Together as we seek God to accelerate our work and mission.

It is astonishing how God orders our steps and aligns our life. I'm humbled to serve this team and to reach new daring destinations together.

REFLECTION QUESTIONS

1. Have you experienced prejudice or bias in the marketplace? How have you healed from those experiences?

2. Have you seen God's purpose in your painful experiences? If so, what is it?

3. What are your personal and mission statements?

4. How are you intentionally leading others? What unique investment do you bring?

5. How would you describe your leadership style? Are you a dare-to-serve or Level 5 leader? How do you know?

6. Define your next daring destination vocationally. What are you prayerfully envisioning it to be?

CHAPTER NINE

TRANSFORMATIONAL MENTORSHIP

Do not conform to the pattern of this world,
but be transformed by the renewing of your mind.
Then you will be able to test and approve what God's
will is—his good, pleasing and perfect will.

ROMANS 12:2

WHEN DESCRIBING SOMEONE'S IDIOSYNCRASIES, my mom usually says, "We all come a certain way." Our family background and subsequent worldview shape our character. Often, what's important to our loved ones becomes important to us as a result of our expressed love for them. The same could be said of our viewpoints. We might adopt a certain thought pattern relative to our ethnicity, gender, or religion; this determines what we value. This pattern of thought informs the questions we ask when we meet others: Where are you from? Do you have any siblings? What do you do for a living? Where did you go to school? The answers we receive paint a picture of the person and whether or not we have things in common. Within a few minutes of meeting someone, we often make snap judgments about who we think this person is based on our cultural norms.

Jesus upended the notion of viewing life through cultural norms when he established the kingdom of God. In God's kingdom we have the capacity to be transformed into the image and likeness of God (Romans 12:2) rather than being defined by our culture or our past. This transformation begins through faith in Jesus Christ and continues as we strive to emulate Jesus' life.

In the Old Testament, God established through Moses his laws and commandments for the nation of Israel. Yet Israel continually rejected the commands of God and opted to live according to their own terms. So God, who deeply loves his creation, sent his Son Jesus to address the sin separating humanity from himself while also modeling a godly life for humanity. Thus, Jesus served as the first example of transformational mentorship.

A mentor is "a trusted counselor and guide" and mentorship is the "influence, guidance or direction as given by a mentor." Jesus, knowing his life on earth would be short and possessing the eternal perspective that through his life would come the salvation of many, understood that his life would have a far greater impact if he directly invested in people. He identified and mentored the twelve disciples.

The disciples went everywhere Jesus did. Through his example and delegation, they learned about preaching and teaching as well as how to heal the sick and cast out demons. They also learned to serve others. They experienced the provision of God as they traveled from town to town.

One of Jesus' first disciples was Simon Peter, a fisher. After performing a miracle that allowed Peter and his fellow fishers to catch a large number of fish, Jesus proclaimed that Peter would fish for people (Luke 5:10). Jesus believed in Peter as a future leader of his church. Peter was one of three disciples (the others being James and John) who witnessed some aspects of Jesus' life that the others didn't see (like Jesus' transfiguration

[Matthew 17:1-6]). Yet he knew Peter would one day deny him (Matthew 26:34). Knowing this, Jesus still chose to mentor Peter.

Prior to the denial of Jesus by Peter, Jesus said to him, "Simon, Simon [Peter's Hebrew name], Satan has asked to sift all of you as wheat. But I have prayed for you, Simon, that your faith may not fail. And when you have turned back, strengthen your brothers" (Luke 22:31-32). As Jesus predicted, after he was arrested, Peter vehemently denied knowing his beloved mentor three times (Matthew 26:69-75). But Jesus eventually reinstated Peter. Three times Jesus asked Peter if Peter loved him. With each yes that Peter replied, Jesus told Peter to feed his lambs, to take care of his sheep, and to feed his sheep (John 21:15-19). Jesus was intentional to provide Peter with instructions for his future. Jesus empowered Peter to a greater purpose than Peter imagined.

We can do the same for those we mentor.

PERCEIVING, BELIEVING, AND EMPOWERING

Some of us have had mentors who said we were the next person to take their job or leadership role even though we didn't believe it was possible. Transformational mentors have an uncanny knack for this type of leadership. Igniting our vision and the belief that we've been called to something greater than we're currently experiencing is a sign of true mentorship.

Our ability to sense and perceive the new thing God wants to do in another person's life is critical as we help a mentee establish a leadership identity.

We *empower* others when we provide them with the truth that becomes a catalyst to more revelation from God. For the mentee acceptance of this truth often takes time. This was evidenced as Jesus mentored his disciples. He instructed them, knowing that their acceptance of their role would be incremental. But they would have an ally—the Holy Spirit—who would provide them with further revelation.

Being mentored teaches us how to steward assignments we might one day be called to possess. In defining life moments like these, the voice of our mentor will push us to accomplish tasks we feel totally unqualified to conquer.

I experience the most joy when I am adding value to leaders and environments while drawing from my personal and professional experiences. I love helping younger leaders uncover their leadership gifts, and I love bringing order to every environment where I have influence. I endeavor to elevate the vision of leaders in the workplace. I help them think beyond what they have been hired to do and to embrace their roles by asking themselves, *What do I want people to remember me for when I'm gone?*

When we view our lives through the lens of the impact we want to make, we can more easily decipher how to intentionally spend our time accomplishing personal and vocational goals. With any mentoring relationship we must leave room in our hearts for disappointment. Our mentee might fail in one area or another, as Peter failed Jesus. Part of our balanced investment in their lives involves preparing them to rebound *after* failure, just Jesus did for Peter.

Let's look at another example of transformational mentoring.

IN THE TRENCHES

Ernie Johnson Jr. is one of the most recognized voices in sports broadcasting. I've watched Ernie on the TNT television network analyzing the NBA for as long as I can remember. I turn to him when I want to hear good commentary on my favorite NBA teams.

In Ernie's book *Unscripted*, he shares that he identified as Catholic but hadn't opened a Bible in a quarter of a century. After being challenged by his children to attend church on Sundays like their school-aged friends, Ernie and his wife, Cheryl, began to attend Crossroads Community Church (now 12Stone Church). Soon after they started attending Crossroads, as Ernie described, God started messing with him. Ernie asked the church's pastor, Kevin Myers, to have lunch with him to discuss what was stirring within him. During this lunch meeting on December 10, 1997, Pastor Kevin led Ernie in a prayer to accept Jesus Christ as his Savior.

As Ernie began to grow in his faith, his wife remained skeptical. While Ernie committed his life to Christ, she wanted to learn as much as she could before committing her life to Christ. Ernie's transformation accelerated, which could be seen though his attempts to clean up his language and his regular visits to Family Christian Bookstores. His wife, however, wondered if he was the same guy she married.

Pastor Kevin invested time, prayer, and encouragement in his relationship with Ernie and Cheryl. But as Ernie writes,

> We hit brick walls. And we obliterated some. And we agreed to disagree on some things, but on others there was firm common ground that steadied us, like the belief that this life isn't all there is. . . . It was that eternal perspective that for Cheryl trumped all those things she was struggling to wrap her head around.

Four months after Ernie, Cheryl accepted Christ.

Pastor Kevin's transformational mentorship resulted in a radical change in the foundation of their faith. Instead of their marriage becoming fractured by the burgeoning faith of one, God redeemed them both. Pastor Kevin got into the trenches with Ernie and Cheryl and wrestled with them in what they believed about God and his will for their lives and family.

Transformational mentorship is deeply sacrificial. It may push us past our comfort zones to walk into the deep with those searching for meaning. Ernie identified Pastor Kevin as his spiritual mentor and his go-to source when faced with other adversities in life, particularly his cancer diagnosis. Pastor Kevin helped Ernie wrestle with "Trusting God . . . Period," a title in his book and the final sentence in his email signature to this day.

Ernie's faith has been on display to the sports world. Like many others, I have taken pride in Ernie's public demonstration of his faith. But what gives me even greater joy is knowing that the investment of his spiritual mentor has influenced many lives.

We may never know the ripple effect of our mentorship and how it might transform lives beyond that of our mentee, yet our investment in another life has the propensity to outlive us.

EMPOWERMENT IS KEY

Transformational mentorship is the crux of leadership across every sphere of society. In his book *Leading at a Higher Level*, Ken Blanchard writes, "Empowerment is the creation of an organizational climate that releases the knowledge, experience and motivation that reside in people." He goes on to say, "Empowerment requires a major shift in attitude. The most crucial place that this shift must occur is in the heart of every leader." Mentorship is transformational because it empowers people, releasing them to invest significantly in the success of other people, ministries, and organizations.

In October 2015, my friend and then colleague Pastor Annette Cutino introduced me to her close friend Pastor Chermain Lashley, then senior pastor of Kings Highway United Methodist Church in Brooklyn (now senior pastor of Grace United Methodist Church in Queens). Pastor Annette was scheduled to be a guest speaker for Pastor Lashley's upcoming women's retreat but couldn't attend because the retreat conflicted with her daughter's birthday celebrations. She recommended me as a guest speaker instead, and Pastor Lashley invited me to come, though we hadn't yet met. This relationship and invitation changed my life.

The retreat was at Tuscarora Inn Retreat and Conference Center in Mount Bethel, Pennsylvania. My best friend, Brandy Anderson, traveled with me. I preached based on the retreat theme, "Woman, Rise from Pain to Power!"

In Pastor Lashley I witnessed a leader immersing her life in the spiritual empowerment of her members. I was mesmerized by her deep commitment. She was completely invested in each woman's pain and victory. I marveled at her exuberance in worship and in one-on-one prayer ministry (no matter how long she labored with someone), the compassion with which she ministered for hours, and the intentionality of meticulously seeking God's direction for every element of the program. Empowering others was deeply personal for Pastor Lashley. She was committed to everyone's success. As she shared stories of her own brokenness and how God met her in those places, she showed women that weekend how to rise from pain to power.

My relationship with Pastor Lashley has blossomed ever since. I regard her as a sister, mentor, and one of my closest friends. Each year since 2015 she has invited me to be a guest speaker at her retreats for women and youth.

During my first weekend youth retreat at Kings Highway in June 2016, I was blown away by nearly one hundred young people who were passionate about a deeper relationship with God. They worshiped with the same exuberance as Pastor Lashley. I could sense their hunger for God. They desired authenticity in the preached Word. Pastor Lashley delivered! I was further blown away when all of them were present at the 6 a.m. "early power prayer" both days that weekend.

I wasn't accustomed to that. On retreats I was used to morning prayer as being optional and no one felt compelled to go. Yet here were kids as young as eleven worshiping God with tears streaming down their faces as they were empowered by God's presence. Their tenacity for God made me want to be a better disciple of Christ. They gave me life! I eagerly went to "early power prayer" expecting God to speak to me.

While reports indicate the potential mass exodus of young people from the church, that was not true at Kings Highway. Here was an opportunity to reach the largest living generation in the United States—millennials—and Generation Z.

A report commissioned by the Pinetops Foundation discussed the possibility that over forty million young people raised in Christian homes might leave Christianity behind by 2050. I hope that like me, your response to this will be "Not on my watch!" Like Pastor Lashley, you could endeavor to become a transformational mentor in the life of a youth.

Year after year I watched these young adults blossom like flowers. The retreats were indeed transformational, and Pastor Lashley's investment in their lives was not just a weekend experience. Other opportunities came through Tuesday night Bible study, regular leadership training, 6 a.m. prayer on Saturday mornings, Sunday evening prayer line, seasons of fasting and prayer, Sunday morning worship services, counseling sessions, weddings, and funerals. These opportunities released these emerging leaders as small business owners, teachers, retreat administrators, and ministry leaders. All of these opportunities happened without a team of other ordained ministers supporting Pastor Lashley.

Whenever Pastor Lashley is a guest speaker at another church, you'll see young adults with her. I have never seen one person be so sacrificially invested in the life of their ministry, caring for and feeding the sheep of God. (Does that sound familiar?) The fruit produced by the lives of these emerging leaders is a testament to Pastor Lashley's faithfulness. Only eternity will tell the full impact of her investment. Empowerment is key!

VISION IS ESSENTIAL

Being able to perceive the new thing God wants to do in the lives of those we mentor is paramount. The Bible says that "where there is no vision, the people perish" (Proverbs 29:18 KJV). When we don't know where we're going, we run the risk of becoming stuck where we are. Leaders are called to infuse others with vision in this journey God has called us to. Vision is important while serving in ministry and when leading organizations.

In John P. Kotter's book *Leading Change*, he mentions that in a change process there are three important purposes of vision and strategy: (1) vision clarifies the direction for change, simplifying future decisions, (2) vision motivates people to take action, and (3) vision coordinates the actions of different people. Kotter writes, "A good vision acknowledges that sacrifices will be necessary but makes clear that these sacrifices will yield particular benefits and personal satisfactions that are far superior to those available today—or tomorrow—without attempting to change."

In leading others toward transformation, Pastor Kevin and Pastor Lashley had to first cast a vision for what was on the other side of change—*faith, growth, empowerment, and purpose.* Those they invested in had to know that their mentor's commitment to this relational investment was for their benefit because they too would be required to sacrifice for the fulfillment of the vision. This change process would alter the trajectory of their lives.

Transformation is a process in which we co-labor with Christ as a leader. As we embark on transformational mentoring relationships, we must be intentional about the following:

- outline our vision and strategy
- become lifelong learners and invest in our ongoing leadership development
- define how often we will meet with a mentor or mentee for intentional investment
- identify our comfort zones
- examine where we'll have to sacrifice
- commit ourselves to the process of change
- prepare for potential failure
- empower our mentees for change

THE CURRENCY OF TRUST

I've had more mentors than I can count. These relationships were formal and informal. I remember only once asking someone to formally mentor me: Rev. Wendie Gail Howlett-Trott. My other mentorships were possible because I willingly submitted to the investment of that leader in my life. That's key. Mentorship is contingent on trust. I had to know that this leader's heart toward me was pure, that the mentor genuinely had my best interests at heart and was not trying to co-opt God's work in my life, and that this leader would not use me as a means to personal fulfillment and selfish gain.

We have to exercise wisdom to avoid being used by others. Typically, we sense when someone's interest in us is transactional—only tied to what we can do for them. This sort of individual will not be available in times of need but will instead place demands on us to accomplish their goals. Actions speak louder than words.

I was comfortable being vulnerable with my mentors, confiding in them some of the most personal details of my life. I trusted that they would not divulge these details in gossip.

Sometimes the intimate details of my life have been shared with others, and at times some have taken liberties with my information when interacting with people I have talked about to the leader. Both are extreme violations, and if not for the grace of God they can impede our lives.

Healthy mentorship has protective boundaries. Mentors who are concerned about our leadership in public and in private will call out character and integrity issues and demand authenticity. They will not stroke our egos or invite us to take on increased leadership responsibilities if they know firsthand that our lives are full of moral failure. They'll care for our souls and walk with us on the road of redemption and healing.

Healthy mentors will also admonish us to care for ourselves physically, viewing rhythms of rest and refreshment as vital to our leadership. When I asked a leader who worked twelve-plus-hour days how much rest she gets, her response was that she would rest when she was dead. Say what? That's a poor leadership example. Even Jesus observed the Sabbath and demonstrated good boundaries by drawing away from crowds for silence and solitude with God (see Mark 6:31).

Another time when I asked a leader why he never takes a vacation, he told me he couldn't because the demands of his local church ministry were too much. Huh? This also is unhealthy and unbalanced. If the president of the United States can take multiple vacations per year, so can we. Trust me, life will find a way to go on without our phenomenal selves. We'd do well planning a period of rest once per quarter. Healthy transformational leaders model balanced lives. They are not committed to their ministries and organizations to their own or their family's neglect.

Healthy transformational mentorship does not foster co-dependency. Again, the goal of mentorship is empowerment— empowering us to stand in our God-cultivated identity, purpose, calling, and life. The goal of the mentor is not to make mentees a miniversion of the mentor. I've never liked when someone refers to another as their Mini-Me. In most mentoring relationships, learning is reciprocal. As a mentor we grow to value our mentees' investment in our lives.

Serving emerging leaders through mentorship has compelled me to be a better leader. I've realized that if I don't have something to offer my mentee in their pursuit of change, I cease to be effective as a transformational leader. Healthy mentors want mentees to surpass them and go to new places in life, taking on new challenges and experiences. The mentoring relationship is a springboard for actualizing the greater works God has called each of us to do (John 14:12). This causes a mentor tremendous joy. I have seen this firsthand.

LOOK UP!

When I described my transition from Movement.org to PULSE Movement, I didn't share how God strategically used my boss at Movement.org, Craig Sider (president and CEO), to influence my decision making even though he didn't know it at the time.

Craig embodies a deep commitment to the mission of gospel movement in cities, and at every turn he affirmed my value in this work. Craig wanted me to excel in my role, but he was equally committed to my success as a leader. He always asked me where I saw myself along the trajectory of growth in Movement Day Expressions. Using the white board in his office, we'd chart my strengths and passions and our sense of how God was expanding Movement Day Expressions, identifying where potential gaps might be. We were honest and trusted each other with the truth we shared in those meetings. Our assessment of things was healthy and balanced. I felt safe with Craig and knew that he had my best interest at heart.

As we conducted these exercises, it was abundantly clear that God was birthing new gifts in me as a communicator to and connector of people and networks, and that I was most passionate about younger leaders and investing in mentoring relationships. God's plan for my life was taking a trajectory counter to my role as director of Movement Day Expressions. This reality was increasingly becoming a truth I had to wrestle with. Craig never said these words explicitly. But that truth hung in the air like a cloud on a rainy day. I couldn't ignore it. These moments caused me to examine myself and ask God what he was up to.

If Craig only valued who I was as an employee of Movement. org, and not who I was to God, those sessions would not have had the impact they did. Craig had no idea what God was stirring in my heart in January 2019 in what would be our last mentoring session as boss and employee. But his ability to help me *look up* and see God's vision for my life is a moment I will forever cherish. He empowered me to dare to see myself beyond my current job. I am forever grateful that he cared for me as a leader even if it would someday mean releasing me. That was sacrificial.

When I shared with Craig that I was resigning from my role at Movement.org, I could hear the emotion in his voice as he told me how proud of me he was. His emotion was heartfelt and genuine as well as immensely affirming. I cried. Leaving Movement.org was one of the most courageous decisions in my life. I was assuming a role with an organization in another state with leaders I had not yet cultivated the same level of relational depth. All of this required unwavering trust in God.

I think Craig and I both knew the day of my resignation would come, but we didn't expect it that soon. God's timing is never subject to our timetable. During the two-month period between announcing my resignation and my final day at Movement.org, Craig involved me in conversations concerning the future of my role and that of Movement Day Expressions. He allowed me to travel to Austin, Texas, to spend a day with a colleague who would take on the lion's share of my role, because he knew it would be meaningful to both of us. I wanted to end well and see God's work continue. Craig honored that. His mentorship and sacrificial leadership in my life were transformational.

To be used by God as a transformational mentor is one of life's most precious gifts. Investing in people affects nations. Who mentored the most influential leaders in our lives? Who sacrificed so that they could live out God's vision for their lives? I guarantee their mentors modeled selflessness, love, and understanding, people who rebuked them as part of their intentional and caring relationship and their unwavering commitment to their success.

If leadership doesn't cost us something, it's not real leadership. Be on the lookout for the people God divinely aligns with us for transformational investment. Seek God often. Pray much. Be willing to sacrifice greatly to raise up a generation of like-minded leaders who will do likewise. Through our mentorship and leadership investment, may churches, cities, and nations be accelerated to do even greater works!

REFLECTION QUESTIONS

1. How would you describe your current or a past mentor relationship?

2. How might you intentionally engage in transformational mentorship? Who do you sense God leading you to invest in?

3. In what areas, if any, do you need to further develop as a mentor? Evaluate the types of relationships that are common to you, the vocational roles you're drawn to, and the areas of life that you find the most gratifying. These can be indicators of how God can use you in the lives of others.

4. What are some examples of transformational leadership you've observed in your community? What impact did those examples have on your leadership?

5. Where might you need to release a leader to their next daring destination?

CHAPTER TEN

LESSONS LEARNED

*Process precedes accomplishment. Have tenacity
to endure the process, because what you learn
will help you survive when you attain your goal.
If you learn to be patient, you will become
consistent in your pursuit of destiny.*

T. D. JAKES, DESTINY

AS I'VE GROWN AS A LEADER OVER THE YEARS, I've often felt
frustrated by my lack of a fuller understanding of all that God has
called me to do. This frustration sometimes causes me to compare
myself to other people, especially those who seem driven. I
wished I was that laser-focused.

If I'm honest with myself, however, I have just enough revelation for right now, and I've learned to be content with that.
While others take pride in the number of cities or countries
they've preached in, how big their honorarium checks are, who
they know, the networks they're a part of, and the privileges and
perks afforded to them, I sit back and wait for God's marching
orders. Waiting for God's leading is just one of the many lessons
I've learned as a leader. Let me tell you some others.

LESSON ONE: PATIENCE

In our pursuit of uncovering every aspect of our leadership and the places God will call us to invest in, we must be patient with God and ourselves. I've watched people who didn't feel affirmed in their ministerial call prematurely leave good churches to start their own churches. Or I've seen them bounce from one church to another, seeking affirmation for their own life's plan. I've also seen talented people who've resorted to purchasing ministerial credentials online, finding ministers to ordain them, or in other instances simply ordaining themselves so they can pastor churches. It's sad to see all of this maneuvering, without accountability and community, simply to massage their ego. They wanted tomorrow today, ignoring the patience involved in God's process of preparation.

In Ecclesiastes 3 the writer, likely Solomon, proclaims,

> There is a time for everything,
>   and a season for every activity under the heavens:
>   a time to be born and a time to die. (vv. 1-2)

There will be a time for your leadership, your discipleship, your study and preparation, your reprieve. Your job is to know the season you're in according to God's timetable, not your own. Slow down and be patient. Let God do the affirming and equipping. Don't be zealous without wisdom (Proverbs 19:2).

Even Jesus painstakingly followed the will of the Father in the fulfillment of the law rather than serving his own agenda. If Jesus can show patience, we certainly can. It's one of the fruits of the Spirit after all (Galatians 5:22).

LESSON TWO: ENDURANCE

Time and again we will have to endure changing demographics and cultures that will demand that our leadership shift and grow.

Our company has a new CEO and takes a new direction. Our church has a new senior pastor with different expectations for the church leadership team. Our spouse has had an epiphany and now wants to be a vegan after years of a carnivorous lifestyle. Sounds silly I know, but it happens! Change is inevitable, and as a leader we need to demonstrate flexibility.

Endurance requires a lifelong commitment to study and growth as a leader. When we possess a hunger for learning, we'll see value in all people, especially when we expect to glean nuggets of God's wisdom from them. This doesn't mean expecting people to conform to our ways of doing things, but instead we value learning the differing aptitudes of others: how they're wired, what they respond to, how much encouragement they need, and so on.

When we don't embrace endurance, we can stunt our learning by becoming prideful and operating with a sense that we're all-knowing. Most of us know people who consistently reject all truth other than their own. They are unwilling to change. Others avoid or work around them, and eventually they become dispensable because they resist change at every turn, negating their opportunity to grow as a valuable contributor.

Be disciplined. Embrace endurance by learning to adapt and adjust.

LESSON THREE: COMMUNICATE, COMMUNICATE, COMMUNICATE

Whoever coined the phrase *the art of communication* was a genius. Communication is a skill that must be honed daily in personal and professional relationships.

Sometimes we think we've sent a message to someone only to find out we never did. Or we send an email thinking we were crystal clear only to receive a response back with so many questions we want to pull our hair out. We all hear and respond to information differently, which is why the art of good communication requires being meticulous.

When communicating with others, I have had to learn to exhibit graciousness. I'm not perfect, and I misunderstand things at times. Though I think I'm a good communicator, I could certainly be a whole lot better. I miss words in my written communications and do not fully explain my thinking at times.

As vice president of multiplication at PULSE, a number of staff report directly to me. I absolutely love that I get to serve them; however, some days can be mentally exhausting. I spend *a lot* of time communicating—orally and written. I've learned to

- slow down and evaluate whether or not I conveyed what I intended to convey.
- explain my decision making to guard against misunderstandings.
- give clear direction by first thinking through each step of what I'm communicating.
- flag emails and not rush to respond and instead ponder my thoughts, pray, and then give a balanced response.
- have crucial conversations when necessary.
- apologize for any infractions.
- ensure that I have buy-in from key stakeholders in all decision making.

Thanks to Sheryl Sandberg, I've learned that "the ability to listen is as important as the ability to speak." Listening shows that we value what others have to say and care just as much about their thought processes as we do our own. People need to know they've been heard.

Sometimes we can be so locked into proving our point that we devalue others in the process. Strong leaders work diligently to become good communicators, which also involves being good listeners. I've learned to ask questions such as the following:

- Does that make sense?
- What did you hear me say?
- Can we review the next steps we just discussed?

These questions help to identify any misunderstandings immediately before too much time has elapsed.

LESSON FOUR: COMBATING WORKPLACE ENVY

One day I shared with a networking group of professionals that I had received a significant speaking invitation. I was excited to share the news, but was also apprehensive. I didn't want anyone to envy me but also didn't want anyone to hear of this invitation by different means and feel slighted that I hadn't shared. I can still remember the deafening silence. Not one "Congratulations," "That's amazing," or even a "Can't wait to hear it" was offered. Just blank stares and flat emotions. I wasn't looking to be stroked but for someone to share the joy of entering into a new challenging assignment. Their lack of response was sobering yet eye-opening.

I've experienced various forms of envy throughout my life—at school, work, church, among friends and family. Envy is a natural emotion we all experience.

I've caught the gazes of people I've regarded as friends and could see envy in their eyes. I've made my best attempts to shield my accomplishments from the masses and cringe when good things are said about me in large-group settings. In some instances I've received half-hearted congratulatory words from people. And what has been my response? *Thank you, Lord, for opening my eyes. I do not want to be deceived by the intent of those around me.*

Consequently, I've learned that every success in my life need not be shared, but the blessings of my life do not have to remain a secret. And if I choose to share and the response is not what I'd hoped, I pray for God's peace over that person.

King Saul envied the popularity of David when the women compared David's greater success to Saul's (1 Samuel 18:6-9). God's anointing was clearly on David as the soon-to-be king of Israel. As a result of that envy, an evil spirit tormented Saul and cause him to want to kill David. Yet though David had the opportunity to kill Saul, he instead spared Saul's life repeatedly. David maintained that he would not lay hands on Saul—the Lord's anointed. He determined that it was God's responsibility to deal with Saul (1 Samuel 26).

What happens when we surpass our mentors, our favorite leaders, bosses, or friends? Life goes on, though we may have to deal with the consequential emotions of others. We cannot let someone's envy cause us to apologize for what God is doing in our lives—the doors he's opening, and the favor he's shown us. But we can't become prideful either. And if we experience abusive behavior, as David did, run! Let God deal with those who seek to harm us.

David's example is very sobering. I believe God is reminding us not to dwell on what others are doing but to focus more on how we'll respond. God will deal with them. If we care too much about what people think or whether they celebrate our accomplishments or not, we need to question what we truly value. Is it meaningful to have our accomplishments acknowledged by those we're in relationship with? Absolutely! But should our joy and peace be contingent on their doing so? Absolutely not!

I wonder if God uses moments when our accomplishments go unnoticed as a means of keeping us humble. We need to ask ourselves: *Am I content with God's affirmation, or do I need the affirmation of others?* Thinking in this way helps me guard my heart against carrying unnecessary emotional baggage. I want God's affirmation over that of all others.

In some seasons of life, particularly as we grow as leaders and are given new territory to conquer, our relationships may change. God will raise up new cheerleaders and shift other voices. Let him separate the wheat from the weeds (Matthew 13:24-29)! I honor and deeply value the people God has used at various times in my life to be an expression of his love toward me. It's hard to experience growth in relationships and see our relationships with people change. Phone calls lessen, text messages stop, outings don't happen as frequently as they used to. It's okay; it happens. But don't ask others for permission to grow.

LESSON FIVE: CULTIVATE INFLUENCE

Sometime we simply influence others, but at other times we exert authority over them, wielding our title to get them to do what we want. Being influential as a leader trumps being a dictator. Influence is cultivated through relationships, trust, and proven success. Exerting authority over others is more about who has the power and who doesn't.

Garnering influence requires the investment of time. Take time to cultivate credibility as a leader. Showing concern for the people in our spheres of influence—including asking about their families, their likes and dislikes—is a step toward building influence. This is easy to do with friendships, but it is also a professional necessity. If a colleague shares that she has experienced a death in the family, is our first response to stop everything we're doing to offer emotional support? Or do we hand her a tissue and, when she has stopped crying, ask her to stop by your office to discuss a project? That might sound a bit ridiculous, but this is not a farfetched scenario. Some leaders are apathetic and emotionally detached. They care more about the bottom line than they do people. Furthermore, the apathetic leader projects an inept value system onto others and subsequently develops unrealistic and unhealthy expectations.

Here are some reflection questions to ponder as you evaluate your relational quotient:

- Do you respond to others when they're in need or only when convenient for you?
- Do you follow up to see how people are doing?
- Do you interact only with people you feel called to, or do you value all people?
- Do you acknowledge colleagues or churchgoers in the hallways and in the community, or do you pass them by?
- Do you care primarily about getting work done, acknowledging others only when you need them to do something?

How we respond in nonwork-related matters or moments when we're not the upfront leader (preaching, teaching, etc.) builds a mental picture for others about who we *really* are. Influential leadership is all about integrity. Either we have it or we don't.

We are always learning from verbal and nonverbal cues, evaluating how others will potentially treat us. People remember how we made them feel. Stepping into the well with others—in their place of emotional need—will cause them to be more inclined to do the same for us. When we're emotionally distant, people will not know how to act toward us.

Most of us have been so devoted to a leader that we have gone out of our way to help that person. We did so because we valued the person and their investment in our lives, not because they had authority over us.

Influential leaders harness the power to shift people's thoughts and feelings about a subject due to their trust in our leadership and the integrity we've demonstrated as a caring and compassionate person. Titles have nothing to do with it. This level of intentionality in leadership takes a lot of work to cultivate, but it will garner invaluable influence and trust in our relationships. Leaders who do not have this cache of trust rule with an iron fist. It is the only way they can get work done because they did not invest time in building relationships.

As an introverted leader, I've had to discipline myself to engage with people no matter how much I'd like to be by myself. I don't want people to think that I don't care about them.

Some leaders don't know personal facts about their staff. But I don't want to be that type of leader. I don't want to lead from behind the desk or come across like a big bad wolf over email. I would much rather serve with leaders who will go the distance with me, no questions asked, because they know I'd do the same for them.

LESSON SIX: SEEK INTIMACY, NOT FAME

The entertainment industry is full of one-hit wonders whose brief foray into fame later prompts the question Where are they now? And we've all seen celebrities who crashed and burned as they sought what many seek—fame.

I don't consider myself to be popular by any means. I am not a household name, yet I am known by many. The only thing I have done to become known and regarded favorably by others is to first become known and favored in my relationship with God. As an outflow of that relationship, I've tried to be faithful in all that God has called me to do. I acknowledge the jobs in which I've slacked off and the times I wasn't detailed enough (like when I made mistakes as a wedding planner), and the ways I may have let others down. But now that I know better, I aim to live better.

In "Unbreakable Smile," music recording artist Tori Kelly addresses the push and pull of her celebrity status and what being more "successful" might mean—compromising who she is. In the chorus she says, "You're not breaking me." The song is about being uncompromising in how she governs her life as a musician and a Christian. I love her stance.

The allure of fame often goes in tandem with compromise, though fame itself can be fleeting. When tempted to compromise, ask yourself, *What's driving me? What is my goal?* Regarding intimacy with God as more important than fame or accolades is a safety net. Scripture clearly teaches "It is God who judges: He brings one down, he exalts another" (Psalm 75:7).

At the root of compromise is a complete lack of trust in who God has said he'll be for us. We either don't think that our lives are worth the fulfillment of his promises, or we think so lowly of ourselves that we don't believe God will do what he said he would. Both of those scenarios have been true of me. What about you?

I've had to wrestle with what I believe. At one point in my life my decision making proved that I didn't believe what I preached. I needed to be convinced that God would not forget his promises to me and would not put me to shame. Once I accepted this truth, I was able to ask God to forgive me for all of the ways I'd compromised in my faith.

We must wrestle with whatever is trying to push us to lust for fame and a platform. Remember, as God elevated Jesus' platform, Jesus became more of a target to the religious officials. Their envy led to his crucifixion. Of course, all of that was a part of God's plan for humanity, but are we sure we can handle the opposition that comes with elevation?

I made a habit of asking God to hide me under the shadow of the Almighty (Psalm 91:1). As he pushes me forward to places I never thought I would go, I ask him to guard my reputation, to give me the strength to honor his Word, to keep me from lying to myself and compromising, and to help me remain faithful.

Fame comes with a price. As the hymn "It Is Well with My Soul" says, whatever my lot, I want it to be well with my soul.

LESSON SEVEN: WISDOM IS THE PRINCIPAL THING

We become wise when we yield to the truth of God's Word, consistently learning from others and avoiding making decisions in isolation. I don't think I can underscore enough how vital wisdom is for a leader. A haughty leader regards learning from others as a blemish on their intelligence. The humble leader will view the same dynamic as vital as the air we breathe.

As a young adult I was strong-willed in many situations and paid the price for those decisions. I entertained relationships that I shouldn't have and put my life in the hands of people I barely knew. I look back and thank God for his protection throughout my life. I escaped some situations with emotional wounds, yes, but was physically unharmed.

Well-known leaders who have experienced moral failures in some instances have stumbled over issues in their life that were present long before they attained notoriety. When we're honest with ourselves about our areas of weakness, wisdom dictates that we erect boundaries and ask people to reveal to us our blind spots.

Maintaining the liberty and freedom we've found in Christ takes determination and focus. Having wisdom warrants that we simply confront ourselves, wrestling to obtain the truth versus believing the lie. It means making a decision to uphold God's standard in this area of our life instead of giving in to our own desires. With the strength that only God provides, we must wrestle daily with what we believe to yield to the wisdom of his Word.

IT'S TIME TO MOVE!

As I decided to write a few thoughts in my journal before bed one night, I heard God say, *It's time to move!* I knew immediately what he meant as I began to study Ruth 1:20, which says, "'Don't call me Naomi,' she responded. 'Instead, call me Mara, for the Almighty has made life very bitter for me'" (NLT). Naomi, a Jew, and her daughter-in-law Ruth, a Moabite, had returned to Bethlehem following the death of their husbands. Ruth was determined to remain with her mother-in-law and serve Naomi's God. But Naomi was stuck. She couldn't understand why God had allowed such devastation in their lives. She then did what many of us do—give ourselves a name indicative of our emotional state rather than one befitting our destiny. Naomi instructed everyone to call her Mara, which means "bitter."

Because I had feelings of rejection and disappointment following a broken relationship, I had been calling myself a victim. But like Naomi, I had failed to acknowledge that God had rescued me and was positioning me to fulfill my God-directed destiny. It was time to *move!*

Naomi's wise direction to her widowed daughter-in-law allowed Ruth to garner favor with Boaz, her family-redeemer (a close male relative charged with the responsibility of restoration). Boaz later would marry Ruth and they would have a son named Obed. Obed became the father of Jesse and the grandfather of King David. Through tragedy God actually realigned the destiny of Naomi and Ruth, tying Ruth to the lineage of Jesus.

Naomi had not been called bitter by God; instead, he used the hard times to bring about a change that would ultimately benefit the whole world. But the disruption was difficult to handle at first. I know that the disruptions experienced in my life are ushering me into new places. I pray that you would know the same.

I will not be bitter about what I've endured or regard the ebbs and flows of my life as if my mistakes or shortcomings derailed the timetable of God's providence. On the contrary, the sum of my life to the present day has positioned me to reap an unprecedented harvest.

God has spoken. Let's shift together and step into our new season. It's time to move!

REFLECTION QUESTIONS

1. Which of the lessons mentioned in this chapter do you need to focus on more diligently? Why?

2. How have you viewed the hard times of your life? Have you, like Naomi, assigned a name to them or to yourself as a result? What name do you think God would assign to them or to you? Why?

3. What are some of the biggest lessons you've learned in your time as a leader?

NOTES

INTRODUCTION: HOW GOD SHAPES US

1   *study under the instruction of Ms. Roberta Guaspari*: *Music of the Heart*, directed by Wes Craven (Los Angeles: Miramax, 1999).

8   *70 percent of Africans had never heard*: Mfonobong Nsehe, "Five Lessons from Zimbabwe's Richest Man, Strive Masiyiwa," *Forbes*, February 24, 2013, www.forbes.com/sites/mfonobongnsehe/2013/02/24/five-lessons -from-zimbabwes-richest-man-strive-masiyiwa/#4c3978ff12b1.

2. DISCERNING THE TIMES AND SEASONS

26   *Issues of justice, diversity, and reconciliation*: John Perkins, *One Blood: Parting Words to the Church on Race* (Chicago: Moody Publishers, 2018), 19.

27   *I saw the absolute necessity for reconciliation*: John Perkins, "Dr. John Perkins: My Story," TBN, November 14, 2016, www.youtube.com /watch?v=4t8vG4Fu-z0.

3. DEVELOPING YOUR LEADERSHIP IDENTITY

44   *Advance Leadership Intensive*: "Advance Leadership Intensive," homepage of Lead.NYC, accessed October 21, 2019, https://lead.nyc /initiatives.

45   *Leaders must learn to pay attention*: Adam McHugh, *Introverts in the Church* (Downers Grove, IL: InterVarsity Press, 2017), 133.

49   *Michael is the founder of Public Square Strategies*: "About the Author," in Michael Wear, *Reclaiming Hope: Lessons Learned in the Obama White House About the Future of Faith in America* (Nashville: Thomas Nelson, 2018).

49   *Michael Wear's Q talk*: For access to Wear's video, see the Q website at https://qideas.org/about-qmedia.

4. SURRENDERING ALL

54   *Carolyn Wildermuth discovered*: Carolyn Wildermuth, "What Difference Does Scripture Engagement Make?" American Bible Society, February 26, 2019, http://news.americanbible.org/blog/entry/bible-engagement -leadership/what-difference-does-scripture-engagement-make.

56   *Isabella Baumfree/Sojourner Truth*: For more information on Sojourner Truth see "Sojourner Truth," History, August 16, 2019, www.history .com/topics/black-history/sojourner-truth.

58   *Then that little man in black there*: "Sojourner Truth: Ain't I a Woman?" National Parks Service, accessed October 21, 2019, www.nps.gov /articles/sojourner-truth.htm.

59 *Marie-Yolaine Toms in a video endorsement*: See "Leaders Are Made, Not Born," Rapid Evolution, accessed October 21, 2019, http://rapidevolutionllc .com/development/leaders-are-made-not-born, and Marie-Yolaine Eusebe, "'Leaders Making an Impact': Marie-Yolaine Eusebe's Story," Movement.org, May 19, 2012, www.youtube.com/watch?v=c2VOP8Dzgkk.

60 *leaders are not born but made*: Elizabeth Powitzky, "Great Leaders Are Made, Not Born: Six Strategies for Becoming a Better Leader," *Forbes*, May 25, 2018, www.forbes.com/sites/forbesfinancecouncil/2018/05/25 /great-leaders-are-made-not-born-six-strategies-for-becoming-a-better -leader/#5733cf6a28b7.

Students first become ready: "Are Leaders Born or Made? New Study Shows How Leadership Develops," EurekAlert, October 6, 2014, www .eurekalert.org/pub_releases/2014-10/uoic-alb100614.php.

5. GOD'S CALLING VERSUS MY ABILITY

73 *Growth Skills workshop*: "Growth Skills," Cloud-Townsend Resources, accessed October 21, 2019, www.cloudtownsend.com.

6. THE PATH TO YOUR PLATFORM

80 *Regardless of age, regardless of position*: Tom Peters, "The Brand Called You," *Fast Company*, August 31, 1997, www.fastcompany.com/28905 /brand-called-you.

88 *Kevin Kruse described authentic leaders*: Kevin Kruse, "What Is Authentic Leadership?" *Forbes*, May 12, 2013, www.forbes.com/sites/kevinkruse /2013/05/12/what-is-authentic-leadership/#72bf6eecdef7.

89 *Credible leaders walk the talk*: Peter Economy, "7 Powerful Habits for Establishing Credibility as a Leader," Inc., May 22, 2015, www.inc.com /peter-economy/7-powerful-habits-to-establish-credibility-as-a-leader .html.

For a platform that's constantly changing: Joresa Blount, "Don't Buy Fake Followers: 40 Instagram Tools to Build a Real Following," *Forbes*, August 26, 2019, www.forbes.com/sites/joresablount/2019/08/26 /dont-buy-fake-followers-40-instagram-tools-to-build-a-real -following/#4595af1248b5.

7. LEADING IN THE CHURCH

96 *The kind of quitting I'm talking about*: Geri Scazzero, *I Quit: Stop Pretending Everything Is Fine and Change Your Life* (Grand Rapids: Zondervan, 2010), 15-16.

98 *women serving in a senior leadership role*: "National Congregations Study, Cumulative Dataset (1998, 2006-2007, and 2012), Version 2," Association of Religion Data Archives, accessed November 12, 2019, www.thearda .com/Archive/Files/Downloads/NCSIII_DL.asp.

103   *All confrontation is a search for truth*: Susan Scott, *Fierce Conversations* (New York: Berkley Publishing, 2002), 138-39.

8. LEADING IN THE MARKETPLACE

109   *One of the most important facets*: Carla Ann Harris, *Strategize to Win: The New Way to Step Up, or Start Over in Your Career* (New York: Penguin Random House, 2014), 161.

110   *In the context of teamwork*: Patrick Lencioni, *The Ideal Team Player: How to Recognize and Cultivate Three Essential Virtues* (Hoboken, NJ: Jossey-Bass, 2016), 157.

111   *Self-effacing, quiet, reserved, even shy*: Jim Collins, *Good to Great* (New York: HarperCollins, 2001), 12-13.

114   *if you move yourself out of the spotlight*: Cheryl Bachelder, *Dare to Serve: How to Drive Superior Results by Serving Others* (Oakland: Berrett-Koehler, 2015), 2.

117   *Movement Day Global Cities*: For more on Movement Day Global Cities, see its website at https://movementday.com/md-global-cities.

      Movement Day Expressions: For more on Movement Day Expressions, see its website at https://movementday.com/what-is-movement-day.

9. TRANSFORMATIONAL MENTORSHIP

123   *a trusted counselor and guide*: See definitions of *mentor* and *mentorship* at Merriam-Webster's website at www.merriam-webster.com/dictionary/mentor#h1 and www.merriam-webster.com/dictionary/mentorship.

126   *We hit brick walls*: Ernie Johnson Jr., *Unscripted: The Unpredictable Moments That Make Life Extraordinary* (Grand Rapids: Baker, 2017), 139.

127   *Empowerment is the creation of an organizational climate*: Ken Blanchard, *Leading at a Higher Level* (Upper Saddle River, NJ: Prentice Hall, 2007), 68-69.

129   *reach the largest living generation*: Richard Fry, "Millennials Projected to Overtake Baby Boomers as American's Largest Generation," Pew Research Center, March 1, 2018, www.pewresearch.org/fact-tank/2018/03/01/millennials-overtake-baby-boomers.

      forty million young people: Great Opportunity, accessed October 23, 2019, www.greatopportunity.org.

130   *A good vision acknowledges*: John P. Kotter, *Leading Change* (Boston: Harvard Business Review Press, 2012), 72.

10. LESSONS LEARNED

140   *the ability to listen*: Sheryl Sandberg, *Lean In: Women, Work, and the Will to Lead* (New York: Penguin Random House, 2013), 80.

146   *You're not breaking me*: Tori Kelly, "Unbreakable Smile," *Unbreakable Smile*, Capitol Records, 2015.